You Are My Sunshine

By Shirley Gittoes

And

Rosemary Elliott

authorHOUSE®

AuthorHouse™ UK Ltd.
500 Avebury Boulevard
Central Milton Keynes, MK9 2BE
www.authorhouse.co.uk
Phone: 08001974150

First published by AuthorHouse 11/5/2010.

ISBN: 978-1-4520-9768-8 (sc)

*Front cover image: Copyright Alan Karl Photography
www.alankarlphotography.co.uk*

This book is printed on acid-free paper.

Foreword

Every day in the UK, 17 babies are stillborn or die shortly after birth. Every year the lives of over 6,000 families are shattered by the death of their baby. Their journey through grief to a new equilibrium is long and often lonely.

This book tells the story of one mother's journey but, unusually, this is accompanied by her health visitor's perspective.

With great openness and honesty, Shirley describes how joyful anticipation of the birth of her first baby turned to devastation. She gives the reader a unique insight into the long and rocky road she had to travel and the difficulties she experienced during and after two more pregnancies and births.

Rosemary, Shirley's health visitor, describes very eloquently what it is like to accompany a mother through their grief. Her ability to provide sensitive and respectful care shines through as does her determination to offer long-term care.

Together, the authors provide a unique insight into the very special and therapeutic relationship that can be developed between a bereaved mother and a health professional. Nobody can remove the pain that the death of a baby brings. There is nothing anyone can say that will make it better. However, here is proof that with sensitivity and persistence, midwives and health visitors can build trust and really make a difference to the long term wellbeing of families.

Judith Schott 2010

Sands Improving Care manager

Co-author of *Pregnancy Loss and the death of a baby: guidelines for professionals* Sands 2007

Dedicated to

Book One

My best friend and husband Tim and our three beautiful children

Heulwen, Charlie & Joseph. Thank you for shaping my life to what it is today.

A special thank you to my Mum and Dad for their wonderful support and

Clare for still being my friend throughout the long journey.

Book Two

To Shirley and her family. They have taught me a great deal about real courage.

For all the health visitors' who are prepared to 'go the extra mile' to deliver appropriate professional care to grieving families. God bless you!

And to a little Ray of Sunshine who touched my heart.

Acknowledgements

Book One

Rosemary Elliott

Everyone who has been part of my life and though
unnamed are still part of this book.

To all the special friends who have supported me through
the writing of this book.

To all the wonderful health professionals who have
touched my family.

Book Two

I have to admit that although I was the person to suggest to
Shirley that we write a book about our journey together, I
still had to wrestle with my feelings of not being sure about
how helpful I would be within the text of the story itself.
I feel that this story is Shirley and Tim's and it is one that
should be told. I have found that through my career, not
only in nursing but also in health visiting a true story is a
very powerful tool and one that assists others who find
themselves in a professional supportive role.

I remember when Shirley first asked me to talk at the Sands
conference in Builth Wells in 2008, I went through the
same wrestling process because again I had been unsure

about my usefulness. I had suggested that Shirley 'tell her story' with me supporting her. While I suggested that approach, I was well aware how hard it would be for Shirley to deliver Heulwen's story to an audience of professionals and individuals who had also lost an infant at some point in their lives.

However, that is what happened. Shirley delivered a very powerful story with me injecting in my part as it became appropriate. I am sure that a good few people went away with a lot to think about. That conference has been one of the most humbling experiences in my career but it is coupled with shame after hearing some of the stories of loss from attending individuals and the subsequent lack of caring support they experienced from professionals.

During my career as a health visitor, I have had many surprises, challenges and certainly dealt with my fair share of horror stories. However the one thing I can say with certainty is that through that time I have occasionally had the honour to work with individuals, who in their lives and through no fault of their own have had to experience unimaginable pain and anguish because of the loss of an infant. Two such people are Shirley and Tim and this is the story of our journey together.

Contents

Book One   **1**
Chapter 1 The Beginning   1
Chapter 2 Life goes on   19
Chapter 3 Charlie   35
Chapter 4 Joe   48
Chapter 5 The Journey   87

Book Two   **95**
Chapter 1 Introductions   95
Chapter 2 Grief and Pain   100
Chapter 3 Moving Forward   104
Chapter 4 New Beginnings   109
Chapter 5 Troubled Times   114
Chapter 6 Health Visitor / Health Visiting   121

Book One

Chapter 1
The Beginning

Spring 2000

Can't believe this, absolutely amazing. I had been so busy this month it really had not clicked that I was actually two weeks late. Being pregnant had not even come into my mind until I fainted whilst taking parade. I remember getting home from the weekend cadet training and going straight to the bathroom and doing the test. Looking at that second line come visible was so surreal. The excitement bubbled over and I had to tell Tim. He was sitting by the computer, I was barely able to speak for the excitement and light-headedness so I just put the test stick in front of him on the table. I think it took a minute for him to register firstly what it was I was thrusting in front of him, and then the realisation that it was a positive result. Slowly the smile came over his face, I could see that he was pleased, though for Tim the excitement of the pending fatherhood didn't really take hold until further into the pregnancy.

Being quite naive my first port of call was going to the doctor. I didn't know what was expected and whom I was supposed to tell. I went in and the doctor in her normal doctor manner said "And what can I do for you today?" My sheepish response was "I think I am pregnant." Such a silly response for a thirty-year-old who was so pleased to be there and proud to say 'I am pregnant'. The doctor asked what test was used and that the home tests are very accurate and congratulations.

Congratulations... never thought of that being the word to use. At this stage I still have another thirty-five weeks to get through. It was a really nice word to hear, and such a positive word. The doctor then went through with me the basic process of booking in with the midwife and that unless I had any medical problems through the pregnancy I wouldn't have to go to her again. Seemed logical to me, let's be fair midwives were trained in the aspects of pregnancy and obviously the doctors had a lot of trust and confidence in the community staff. So immediately I felt confident and assured that I was being put into the care of some wonderful people.

I had an appointment with the midwife the following week for a booking in appointment. I spent about an hour with the midwife going through so much; past medical history, the here and now, my details and the details of my husband Tim. It all seemed routine. She explained who my community midwives would be and how often I would be seen. We live in a county that does not have a general district hospital, so we discussed which hospital we would like to have babe in. Though the pregnancy wasn't classed as high risk I was over weight according to the BMI charts so she advised me that I would most likely be advised to go to the main hospital, which to be honest was just going over my head. I just went along with everything that was said. I knew she knew what she was on about and she said that there was plenty of time to discuss it with Tim and the midwives again.

My next appointment to see the midwife was a month later. During the month I had suffered from terrible morning sickness. At that stage morning sickness just did not seem the right description to me, as I was sick pretty much continuously throughout the day. I had to tell my boss a lot sooner than I wanted to because I struggled to drag myself away from the toilet in the mornings. I was frightened that I would walk down the street and start heaving again. Not a pretty sight for someone to see. On a couple of days I didn't manage to get to work because I was so bad with the sickness. This was a learning curve for Tim. He felt so unable to help, and being quite a sickly person it took him a while before he was even able to put his arm through the door just to rub my back. I remember one day I was so glad he was there as I was struggling to get a breath through the heaving. He was such a gentle person and soothed me enough to be able to just relax to take that breath. Talk about trying every single old wives tales for morning sickness. None of them really worked, not for me during this pregnancy.

The next few months of the pregnancy were event free. My appointments with the midwife were going fine; I didn't seem to be any different from anyone else, other than constantly sick. We had the Downs Syndrome blood test done, though the rate was high it wasn't what we felt was a concern, 1-200. To us that was fair and even if we were that 1 in 200 we were not able to terminate this much-wanted baby. The appointment with the midwife when she found babe's heartbeat for the first time was such an amazing appointment. I could not believe that this little baby inside of me was already so advanced. I searched for all the information on the foetus that I could find and knew that babe was fully formed and was now growing in size. Life was just so amazing.

With a work colleague we took our final exams for our Dental Nurse qualification in the November. The training we had been doing for the last twelve months. The results I wouldn't receive until after babe was born. Something else I could look forward to.

I continued to work until thirty-six weeks when I was advised by my midwife to finish as my job entailed being on my feet a lot and they were starting to swell noticeably. Babe was due at Christmas, so I finished work at the end of November.

During this month I had a student health visitor come and visit me at home. She wanted to go through the purpose of the health visitor within mine and babe's future. It was nice to know what was going to happen; to know that I wouldn't be just left on my own with a new baby in my arms. That thought did petrify me. Everyone used to say "Don't worry it all comes naturally" I just hoped they were all correct in their thinking. I wasn't as convinced as them.

I was down to weekly visits to the midwife; my due date came and went. The New Year was on us and Tim was back at work. I was walking a bit more now in the hopes it would shift this baby out. I was absolutely huge and at the final stage of being totally exhausted and tired of being pregnant. The consultant had told us that if babe had not made an appearance by the 14th January, then I would be induced. I was so hoping this wouldn't be needed as I had heard that it was more painful if induced.

It snowed over the next few days and I remember Tim every morning going out to check the car started and was defrosted. We didn't want to be caught out. Thank goodness the cold spell did not stay for long. On the 11th January, I went to bed quite early as I had been finding it so hard to sleep. Sleep again did not want to grace me, as within an hour of me going to bed I started to have severe pain in my abdomen. I left it for a while just trying to find some position that was comfortable. No such luck. I called Tim, who was still up watching telly. He came up and sat with me and timed the contractions.

It was weird but I remember thinking that if this was the pain, I have no idea how women kept having babies. It was so much worse than I ever imagined. The contractions were a steady five minutes apart. Tim turned into the doting husband and called the community midwife. She told us to come over to the community hospital. So off we went, the hospital bags in the boot of the car, Tim being the dutiful driver and me trying to hide the fact that this was first stage labour and I was struggling. I was thinking that I must be such a wimp, many have done this before me and many more will carry on. So why was I being such a wimp? I was only having a baby, nothing else.

We arrived at the hospital to be greeted by the midwife on duty. She was wonderful; I explained where the pain was and how regular it was. She checked me over and told me that babe had not engaged so she would feel better if we went to the general district hospital which we had chosen. We knew this would be an hour drive so off we went. We knew the midwife had made the decision so that we were in the safest and best place possible. By the time we reached the hospital the contractions were three minutes apart. The pain was so excruciating and when I tried to explain the midwife was polite but basically told me, what do I expect I am having a baby.

Sadly babe had still not engaged so we were told that it was going to be a while. Now that made me want to scream, how long was a while going to be. How long could I cope with this pain? I remember saying to Tim if they put a zip in my abdomen then babe would just pop out as I could feel it pushing me there as if the down way route was not an option.

We were showed to a room, Tim was shown to the chair in the corner and I was given a sleeping pill to help me get some rest through the contractions. It was about two in the morning by this point so we were both shattered and in need of the down time, if that was possible.

Though a restless night, we both managed to get a couple of hours shut eye. The contractions hadn't changed. They were still between three and five minutes apart. We had some breakfast and tried to keep some light conversation going. Nothing to serious or contractions related. Something to try and take my mind away from the pain. It wasn't for a while that I realised the actual contractions had stopped, but not the pain of the continuous pushing on the abdomen region, I was feeling extremely tender and, if honest, was glad of the reprieve.

I was monitored for the next hour or so. When just after lunch nothing had started up again it was suggested that we go out for a walk. Fresh air, nice thought. They thought with a walk it could start the contractions off again. No such luck. Back in the room babe was monitored again, it was said that babe was showing a good trace and that they would see what the doctor thought when he did his rounds. At around six o'clock the midwife returned having seen the doctor and said we could go home. If contractions start again, go straight there and bypass the community hospital. I did say that my abdomen was still very tender, as, being honest, I was unsure if I was able to go through that pain again. But knowing I had no other choice if I wanted babe to enter this world.

We went home and enjoyed the home comforts of our own bed. The following day I just sat on the sofa having the tender loving care I was so in need of. I was still very sore. Tim's auntie called in to see how I was, I remember telling her that I was so grateful of the reprieve as the pain was unbelievable and it just gave my body time to just ease off the bruising I felt in my abdomen.

The reprieve didn't last for long as later that evening the contractions started again. This time the pain was totally different, it was a bearable pain which was downward. Again timing contractions we did the pacing. I even had a bath to try and prolong the stay at home before the journey to the hospital. After the bath and back into clothes Tim put the tens machine pads on my back. That was quite a relief and I found it very helpful. By 4am we felt that waiting any longer could be silly as we still had an hour's drive. So again off we went. This time we both said this would be the last time we would be only two.

The journey was quite an amusing one. One that even now I still giggle about. It was about halfway there that, with the contractions, I really needed to go to the toilet. The Welsh countryside at 4am just does not provide those types of luxuries. So the next lay-by would just have to do. Now trying to get out of the car and pants down to have a wee was quite a feat. Time the contraction, would have enough time to get out of the car before the next contraction, breathe, ok got through that one now pants down and have a wee quickly before the next contraction, breathe. Now get pants back up and back into the car before the next one. All done, now let's go.

We arrived at the hospital to be greeted by a midwife who we saw for a while on my previous visit. She asked why I was still about and hadn't this babe made an appearance yet. To my obvious giggle and then breathe, she showed us to the labour room. She stayed with me from here on out. She let me walk about for a while, however I was comfortable. The tens machine was doing well. After a while she needed to check my progress, I was only 3 cm dilated. Now after twelve hours of first stage labour, that information was telling me I had a long way to go.

The midwife strapped me up to monitor babe; she saw some irregularities and went to get her supervisor for a second opinion. The other lady said it seemed fine and to watch. They decided that as I had so long to go if I agreed it would be a good idea to have some pethodine at this point. I agreed as I was finding it hard constantly lying down through the contractions. The tens machine had been removed when I had gone onto the monitoring machine and I had to admit it had been doing a brilliant job. So any relief was good now.

Time and exact events became very muddled. I felt that I became quite drugged. I was in the room having the contractions, but I was also floating on a nice white fluffy cloud.

The irregularities with babe's monitoring continued and the midwife asked the doctor to come and check me and babe over. Now this is when a lot of things happened very quickly and Tim has had to help me over the years to fill in the gaps.

When the doctor came she checked the monitor reading of babe and then checked me. I was still only 3cm dilated. They felt that by breaking my waters it would start to speed things up a bit. They broke my waters and due to the maconnium knew that babe was in severe distress. I was now being asked to sign to agree to an emergency caesarean section to get babe out quickly. Obviously I signed, whilst the rest of my body was being prepared for the surgery. They wheeled me down to theatre what seemed likes only minutes after they had broken my waters. A midwife had one of the handheld heartbeat monitors to keep a trace of babe's heartbeat. At one point she lost it, she told us that it's probably just the monitor. She disappeared for a moment. Tim was told that he was not able to go any further and that he would be taken to a waiting room. I said to him not to worry I would be fine.

I was taken into theatre leaving Tim by the door, which was the loneliest time. Tim and I have always been a very close couple, best friends, so to me the time that he should have been there he had to just wait. In those few seconds of being alone it wasn't long before I had a familiar face again. The midwife was there with me, she came straight to me and said don't worry she was there. This midwife was a sudden lifeline to normality. The anaesthetist asked me to count down from ten. I remember hearing the nurse next to me telling him that my blood pressure was dropping, and then I was gone into a stress-free sleep.

I was coming round, couldn't open my eyes yet but I could hear people around me talking. Then I hear Tim's voice. I had to hear what they were saying. The voice next to me said "Does she know?" know what, what was I supposed to know? Then Tim was there again I could feel him there. He asked them if I was coherent enough to hear him. Now I had to open my eyes, I knew Tim needed to say something, and he was not himself. I opened my eyes and there was Tim in my view. He had been crying or if not crying he had those red eyes as if he was holding back.

"Where's my baby, what did we have?" I had loads of questions to ask him but those two where the first that came through my lips.

"Hun, we had a little girl, but she didn't make it." No, this is not supposed to happen, pregnancy means baby.

I heard screaming, I wasn't there it wasn't happening to me. It was a while before I realised the screaming was coming from me. It was me who was howling, I could not stop myself. Tim was holding my hand now and trying to give me a hug to comfort me. I had a mask on my face and I wanted it off, it felt like I was being smothered. With Tim close by they took us back to the room we had in the labour ward when we had come in three nights previously.

For a while there were people running around us checking this wire and that wire, this drip and that bag. I didn't recognise any of the midwives; all I wanted was my mum. If mum was there she would make me feel like that child again and this would never have happened to us. Tim did not want to leave me but sadly someone had to make those phone calls that everyone was waiting for. For the first time in our lives we were alone together. I knew Tim had to make those calls but I didn't want him to have to be alone either.

Tim went outside to call all the people on the list, though the list had suddenly been shortened the obvious needed to be done.

Tim first rang my parents and spoke to my mum, they were on their way. Then he ran his parents, my mother-in-law was totally shocked and all she said was "That happened to us". Suddenly Tim was not only grieving for his daughter but finding out that he had a sister too.

He made the duty phone calls to the immediate friends and left them to call around to other friends. By the time Tim came back up to the room he was exhausted from trying to tell people without breaking down himself. The typical man trying to stay strong, but that isn't Tim. He is not that hard man; he is a loving gentle man. We spent some time talking about all the calls he had made. Whilst we were chatting and crying a midwife came in. She had two photos of our daughter. We had decided to give her the name which we had chosen for a girl, Heulwen, Welsh for 'sunshine'. The midwife asked us if we wanted to see the photos, of cause I did, I wanted to see and hold her.

The midwife went and got Heulwen to bring her to us. We held and cuddled her. I held her so tight I didn't want to give her back. If I will it surely she would come back to me. It just couldn't be real. I had followed all the rules of pregnancy, what did I do wrong? I couldn't stop the tears. All the last nine months were for this moment. The moment that every parent enjoys. The holding of my daughter, but my daughter didn't cry, she didn't move. She was just so cold, perfect in every way, but silent.

We knew that my parents would be here soon and didn't know how they would feel about meeting Heulwen. So she was taken to the room next door. It was not long before mum and dad got there. I could hear my dad's voice outside and they were shown in. Mum came straight over to me and gave me that much needed mum hug, I couldn't stop the tears, and mum couldn't make it better. I knew she would if she could, but for once in her life she had to just be there. No one could make this go away.

Dad went straight to Tim gave him a hug. Dad could see that Tim was trying to be the strong one, Tim had cried with me but hidden it from everyone else coming into the room. Dad just said "it's ok to cry". The next hour we were telling mum and dad everything that happened, and then the big question, "would you like to meet your granddaughter Heulwen?" I remember being so frightened that they would say no. Neither said that they were just waiting for us to ask them. They didn't want to upset us by asking.

Heulwen was brought back into us; granny and granddad had their time holding their granddaughter. Tim took photos of them with Heulwen; I didn't want to forget her, or the people who held her close. Dad took a couple of pictures of Tim and me with Heulwen our 'family picture'. Tim even now thought himself silly that he smiled for the photo. He knew it was so sad but he was also very proud to be Heulwen's daddy. Something even death could never take away.

When mum and dad went we were alone again, just the two of us with our silent daughter. We had decided that we would remember everything we could today and then not see her again. Not because I didn't want to but more because even now she was deteriorating and I wanted to remember her with the pretty face, dark curly hair just like her daddy. Her beautiful perfect hands. It was whilst we were alone that we cried until we thought we had no tears left, but more still came. That night after the whole afternoon with Heulwen, Tim put her back into the Moses basket and tucked her in and said "Good night and goodbye my little angel."

Tim stayed in the chair next to me that night; we couldn't cope at this stage independently. We seemed to cope better at this stage together. Tim could pre-empt me and vice versa. Our night was a slow one, we talked, cried and slept. I was still on morphine for the pain which was quite helpful. Not that it eased the pain in my heart and soul. I did not know how I was going to cope without my daughter with me. Our whole year was planning our future, the future which involved our child, our much-wanted daughter.

The following day Monday 15th January, was non-descript. We woke, we cried and we slept and in between all of that we talked a lot. During the late morning the midwife came in and told Tim that he needed to register Heulwen with the births and deaths register and told him where to go and not to worry as she would stay with me. As soon as Tim was out of the door that was it, time to get me moving. She seemed to know what would pull my strings and told me I had to get myself out of bed as Tim was so worried about me. I didn't want Tim worrying any more than he already was. So with a lot of help I was moved out of bed and into the chair that Tim had slept in the night before. How he slept now amazed me as the chair was not one of the most comfortable ones. It was amazing how much just the move from bed to chair had not only exhausted me but made me feel slightly in control of what was happening.

When Tim walked back into the room his smile was so special. It was as if he was so proud of me. He came over and sat next to me and told me what had happened when he registered Heulwen. It was a special moment for him but one he had wished we could have done together. I had been so proud of him; he was being so strong when I knew he was breaking into a thousand pieces. The midwife from Heulwen's birth called in to see us, she was on her day off and didn't want us to be moved back nearer home without seeing us. She asked us if we wanted to know anything. Some things they remember better than us. She sat and chatted to us and went through the events of the previous day just to fill in the blanks. This midwife was a special part of Heulwen's existence and a person I would remember for a long time.

I moved back into bed after lunch as the exertion of moving had drained me both emotionally and physically.

We had visitors during the afternoon. Tim's parents came to see us. They were totally consumed with their own grief at the death of their granddaughter. They were also revisiting the grief felt at the death of their own daughter, which at the time they were unable to express openly.

That evening we agreed that Tim needed to go home, he was exhausted and needed to have a proper bed. I didn't want him to go but knew it had to be for the best. Tim needed a bit of down time for himself. We had gone over everything again and again. Tim needed to get home and have a soak and a night's sleep. He promised to be back in the morning.

Once Tim had gone I remember how quiet it all seemed. There were the baby monitors beeping in the ward, which made me cry. I could hear everyone outside my room. So everyday, none of them realise that what is supposed to be so natural doesn't always work out. I eventually cried myself into a restless sleep. Waking only to find my pillow wet, and to feel that I was still crying.

The following morning my consultant came to see me. Tim had not arrived yet and I was worried I would forget something. He went through everything he knew with me and then spoke about a post-mortem. I did not want Heulwen cut up, but I had to wait and discuss it with Tim. Where was he, why was I so alone going through these types of questions? The doctor told me not to worry as he would come back and chat to Tim as well once he arrived. He asked me before he left if there was anything I wanted to ask him. I did, I wanted to ask why? But he had already answered the why, so why me? But no one can answer that. So I said "please, don't let this happen to us again". What a stupid statement to make! His response was so perfect I couldn't ask for any better.

"I will do everything in my power not to let it happen again".

When Tim came in, the consultant returned and spoke to him, giving him all the information he had given me earlier. I didn't have to try and remember it; Tim was here now. Once our consultant had left the room we talked about the post mortem and though I was really not happy Tim convinced me that it was a good thing; even if it can't help us, it could help someone else or us in the future. So we agreed that Heulwen would be sent to Cardiff for her post mortem.

Because of the distance from home we managed to get it agreed that I move to the community hospital for the remainder of my postoperative care. So, later that day, trying to muster all the strength left in me I walked out of the hospital where my daughter still lay.

We travelled back to the local hospital with empty arms .

I cried most of the way back; I felt like I was leaving my little girl unprotected, alone and unloved. Even the bumps on the road back were nothing compared to the pain I was feeling for deserting my little girl. Empty arms, shattered dreams.

We arrived at the local community hospital about an hour later to find a midwife waiting at the door for us. After the journey and the emotional draining I felt unable to walk; it was like all the energy I had left in me was used to get out of the main hospital leaving Heulwen behind. The midwife had a wheel chair there and she took me up to a private room. She was crying with me and I felt she didn't have to say a word because her tears were saying it all. She was feeling it with us. She stayed and got us settled in the room and made sure Tim was doing alright as well, which meant a lot to me. It was me in the bed and in pain, but Tim was still Heulwen's daddy and was grieving too. He was also feeling the pain by seeing me in the bed struggling as I was.

The remainder of the week I stayed in the local hospital building my strength up again. I suddenly had to cope with the visits of friends. Some would come in and couldn't say much of anything; at least they tried to be there. It was good to know that they were there to support us both. One visitor had us both smiling, which had been the first smile that had crossed our faces in the week.

A friend who had three young children called in. She said that she couldn't leave the children anywhere so they were with her. It hurt me to have to be confronted with children so quickly. Her heart was in the right place; the bit that made us both giggle was she then said "We got you some grapes, but we ate them for you on the way". Laughing made me hurt, but it was so amusing.

On the other scale a senior medical person working in the hospital came in one evening and chatting to me, saying she understands and then the crunch sentence "well you are young enough to have more". More! I didn't want more. I wanted my daughter and only my daughter. How was I to know at this stage if I could cope with another pregnancy? I was sure if I had had the strength to argue I would have done. It just hurt me so much that I rolled over to end the conversation and then cried my eyes out again. Would I ever stop crying, would the pain ever go away?

I didn't want the pain to go away I just wanted to have my daughter again, just hold her again. I was so frightened that I would, could forget what she looked like. What she smelt and felt like.

I was allowed to leave the hospital on the Friday; I still had to take a lot of pain relief and antibiotics because I had got a nasty infection from the surgery. So we went from the hospital to the chemist. I did not want to stay in the car on my own. The community in which we live is quite a close knit one, so if I had been seen they would have come over to talk. I couldn't do that alone. So I walked to the chemist with Tim to collect my prescription. It was obvious how news travels so fast. We walked down the street and already people crossed the road away from us. I wanted to shout and scream at the world. We went into the chemist and handed over the prescription to the girl behind the counter. Normally it would take a while for them to do the medications up. Not today. The pharmacist was wonderful and within a couple of minutes he came back out and handed the prescription drugs over. He asked how we were doing. So genuine.

We went home from there and that is where I stayed without going out for over a week. I couldn't face the world, the people or the children. I was jealous of all those parents who could never understand that things can go wrong. Just seeing them with their children made me see how inadequate I was. I felt that it had to be my fault. Why hadn't I made the doctor from our first visit come and see us before he went off? If only I had told him myself the pain I had been in from those first contractions. Was that when Heulwen had first been in distress?

The midwife came to see me on a daily basis once I was out of hospital. The wound from the surgery was not healing as they had hoped it would and by the tenth day the midwife had to remove an inner stitch so that the hole that was remaining open could close and heal properly.

My only contact with the outside world was the contact I had with these midwives, they were my lifeline at this stage. Tim was still home. I was finding it hard to be alone, or more like away from Tim. I found the prospect so emotional that the anxiety levels went so high I was having quite bad anxiety attacks. Logic told me I knew what it was but emotions just couldn't seem to stop them.

We wanted to arrange Heulwen's funeral ourselves. We needed to do the only thing we could for her and that was to place her somewhere local where we could visit her. It was a week after Heulwen died that the local Canon came to see us. We talked about what we would like for our daughter's final resting place. He said he had chosen a special place for her already. Under a large tree which was close to the front of the church, where the sun shines all around her, but she is shaded from the heat of midday. Just what we wanted for her. We could not arrange the exact day of the funeral at this point because Heulwen had not yet returned from Cardiff. As soon as we get any news back we could let him knew and a date and time for Heulwen's funeral could then be arranged.

We found out that Heulwen was still in Cardiff and arrangements could now be made to have her brought home. She was coming home. The funeral director travelled to Cardiff and brought our daughter back to the local chapel of rest. I wanted to see her, just one last time. It was so hard because Tim really didn't want me to go. He was concerned that seeing her after the post mortem and so long after she had died would be too traumatic for me. So I never did. Her funeral was arranged for the following Monday afternoon. Two weeks and one day after she had died.

The funeral day arrived, a day of so much emotion. Tim collected the flowers. We chose a teddy bear cushion of white flowers, with two yellow roses in its hand so we could give them to Heulwen before she is gone from us forever. We had felt most comfortable with the colour yellow because of her name. Heulwen is our sunshine angel, so yellow suits her. We went to the church with my mum and dad, they had come early to give moral support both for us and themselves.

We met everyone outside. We kept the funeral very small with immediate family and very close friends only. We didn't want others there. It didn't feel right to me. I was trying to not cry, needed to be strong for Tim. We all walked into the church together as one big family. Tim and I were holding each other up. I was searching for what felt like ages, I couldn't see her, couldn't see her small white coffin on the tiny white altar. I had sat down before I actually saw her tiny coffin. I was trying so hard to be strong, but seeing her tiny coffin sat there next to the candles and the cross and listening to the Canon it felt like it was all a blur, nothing seemed to be going in. I wasn't there in my mind. Then I heard him telling what seemed to me a story. The significance of lighting the candle to light her passage. Now I heard that. Now I know why they always light candles.

Heulwen's service in the church came to an end. This was Tim's moment, something he wanted to do for his daughter. The last thing he could ever do; carry her to her final resting place. Tim walked ahead holding Heulwen in her coffin, so gently and with so much pride. Strong arms seemed to walk me forward. It was my mum guiding me through. For a short woman (who I have many a time thought of as fragile) she was the strength to hold me up. I could not see for the tears, I am not sure if I truly wanted to see. I still did not want to believe that I would never ever see my daughter again.

Ashes to ashes, dust to dust......clunk. The soil landing on her sweet coffin was echoing. It was my turn now, I had to walk over to the edge of the deep hole and look down. I kissed the yellow rose and dropped it down to her; through my tears I could hear the squeak as I said my goodbye to my sunshine angel.

Chapter 2
Life goes on

30.01.2001

The day after Heulwen's funeral Tim had to return to work. Just the thought of this was frightening me. I had not been able to answer the door to anyone, (in fact unless I was expecting them I used to hide). As for the phone it had been very rare that I had answered it. Generally Tim had done it all. So how was I going to cope? What happened if someone started to ask questions which at this point I was not able to answer? I could not say to them I know I caused my daughter's death. I must have, she was too perfect to have died for no reason. The morning Tim went to work I was shaky, but for Tim I had to be strong. I had to let him be able to go to work without worrying about me.

By four o'clock I was so anxious and in need of Tim's calming nature that a small alcoholic beverage became a necessity to calm my frayed nerves. I knew that logically I had no reason to be scared. I remember trying to work out what I was scared of and why it was mainly focused around Tim. It took a lot of soul searching to eventually work out why. I just could not cope with the death of my daughter and the fear of something happening to Tim was totally unbearable. So now I thought I had worked out my emotional faults could I actually be able to put them in check? Maybe another little drink will surely help me out.

I have never been a drinking person; even in my youth I was never much of a drinker. So a need to have a drink was quite alien to me. The thought of a drink helping me sleep was a refreshing thought and one I needed to feel in control of to explore. Even when totally intoxicated it did not really aid my sleep. Would it help me tomorrow night?

The midwife called around to check that the scar was healing properly now. She also told me that the health visitor would be calling me over the next few days. I had no idea what a health visitor could do, Heulwen wasn't here. The day passed slowly.

During this week once Tim had gone to work, my closest friends visited. One of my very closest friends was also pregnant. We had gone through the pregnancies together. Though she had been to see me in the hospital and at Heulwen's funeral I had shut out the fact that she was still happily pregnant. It was today that she called in to see me. I tried to stay positive for her. She doesn't need me to be down or worrying her. She was due any day now.

My friend was trying her best to cover up her bump. I asked how everything was going. I thought I wanted to know. I was jealous; I wanted it to be me still pregnant. I could never tell her how much seeing her hurt me so badly. She was like a sister to me. We always had a feel of each other's bumps kicking. My baby would never be kicking me again. One day, my friend asked if I wanted to feel her baby moving. It felt like it was rubbing salt into an open wound. Why would I want to do that now. When we were both pregnant that was fine, but things had changed, now my sweet beautiful Heulwen was dead. I loved my friend as family, but right at that moment I hated the hurt and pain that her presence was making me feel. For the first time in my life, I was actually relieved when she went home, as I was then able to cry for what should have been.

It was over the next couple of days when I had a phone

call from the health visitor. It wasn't the student health visitor who I had seen before Heulwen was born, it was Rosemary. Rosemary explained that she had taken over the case because of the exceptional circumstances. I was still under midwifery care at this point but Rosemary wanted to arrange a time to come and visit me. Now that wasn't a problem, I wasn't going outside of my door. So I was always home. I still did not want to go out and see people. I couldn't deal with the looks or the whispers. I knew it was going to come, but not yet.

Hopefully if I left it long enough people would forget. Arrangements were made for Rosemary to come over. I had no idea what she could do, but she had said on the phone that her job is to care for mother and baby. I wasn't sure how I felt about a stranger coming over but I could not say no at this point. I didn't have the emotional strength to say anything bad.

Nighttime seemed to be getting ever harder; the day seemed to pass at a normal pace. If I wanted it to go quickly I got on and did something. Even the smallest of chores seemed to take me forever. Why was I feeling so tired all the time? Not a day had yet gone past without me breaking down in a heap. I have always been a very strong and organised person, knew what I was doing on a day-to-day basis. Now I could not even make food without wrecking it. Why should this happen to me? Suddenly my life had collapsed because my daughter had died; I needed to grieve but I just did not know what was right or wrong. I did not realise that grief was so painful.

Rosemary's visit seemed to come round very quickly and the day was here. I was beginning to feel the anxiety building up. I had to see a stranger, someone who knew me and what had happened but I only knew her as a health visitor. I was getting myself so worked up and even walked to the phone to call and cancel the appointment. Just could not lift the phone to do it. The appointed time was upon me too soon, when I heard the creak of the gate opening I felt like I was shaking so much I wouldn't be able to open the door. Then came the knock, even though I was expecting it the sound still made me jump. Here goes, time to be strong and put that brave face on.

I opened the door to a motherly-type person who introduced herself as Rosemary. Still very shaky I opened the door just enough to let her in. Outside the front door was such a scary place for me right now. Did not want it to come in the house and invade my safe haven. Rosemary could see straight away without me saying a word how nervous emotionally I was at that moment. In a very professional way without breaking my safe haven we both sat down. Now this is stupid I had forgotten my basic manners because of my emotional state. I offered Rosemary a cuppa. Her next actions were what started to build a bit of trust. It wasn't me that made the cup of tea, Rosemary asked if I would mind if she made the drinks, and that was exactly what she did.

Rosemary stayed for over an hour on that first visit, we talked about Heulwen and what had happened. Rosemary didn't push me for answers; I told her the bits I wanted to talk about. It was a strange feeling because this lady whom I had just met was not looking at me with those sympathetic eyes, or finding it hard to make conversation. She spoke to me as an adult as someone who just needs a friend, she never forced me to speak or asked me to open up or invade the safe zone where my mind and body was. I only spoke of the parts where I was not to blame. I couldn't talk about the parts which were my fault. It had to be my fault; no one else could have been to blame.

Before Rosemary left she arranged to call in to see me on the first day that a midwife would no longer be seeing me. It meant that no day would go by without someone calling in. I actually felt reassured about this as I wasn't sure I wanted to break the connection of a daily visit. Someone who knew that Heulwen was a real baby, my daughter, not just a figment of my imagination.

That day came soon enough; I was no longer under the care of the community midwife. The thought of loneliness was ever stronger. I was so thankful knowing Rosemary would be calling. Tim and I always talked but I was struggling with him being emotionally able to go to work. It made me feel that he was no longer grieving, though I did *know* he was. It was that our grief and the process of grieving were taking different paths.

It was in the first week of Rosemary visiting that the most emotional event happened. My best friend gave birth to a healthy baby girl. I should have been so overjoyed for her and being able to wish her the best for the future with her new daughter. I could not do it. It felt like someone had just stabbed me in the back with a knife and was now twisting it.

I knew she would want me to go and see her and her daughter, but how could I? Would I be able to hold her or would I turn away? These emotions were not something I could deal with as they were too powerful for me to be able to accept so soon after Heulwen's death. On the other hand how could I let my best friend down? How could I let her daughter's safe arrival be marred by my grief and jealousy? Tim wanted me to go and see her as he felt it would help me. (Though help me to do what I was not sure, maybe to become more depressed within my own grief?)

Rosemary came into her own with me during this time, she understood the emotional tearing I was feeling and was even able to put into words what I was too scared to speak out loud. "Why would I want to see her baby when all I actually want is Heulwen"

With Rosemary's support I arranged to visit my friend in hospital, with her I even arranged a time and she would ask no one else to visit at the same time. She was trying so hard to understand and make the first visit as bearable as possible for me. Rosemary would visit me later in the day just to make sure I was alright and talk over the visit.

The day came and I went up to the hospital. Now bearing in mind I had to go out of the house which in itself had been an ordeal, I then drove up to the hospital for the first time since the surgery. So I was shaking before I even got to the hospital because of all the firsts I have achieved in one day. I then had to walk to the maternity ward the room next to where I stayed on my return to the local hospital. I walked into the room and saw her. I could not look into the crib for a few moments; I needed to just get my bearings for a moment. She was alone I walked in, her eyes even though she was overjoyed with pride held the sorrowful depth of knowing how hard this was for me.

The time had now come when I had to actually look inside the crib, I could not put it off any longer. Her daughter was lying in the crib, so quiet. Not the deathly quiet of Heulwen, but a quiet of anticipation. Her little eyes seemed to be looking out at the movements surrounding her. Then those words which I was dreading 'you can pick her up if you want to'. I could feel the first bout of tears filling my eyes. I had tried so hard to be strong and save the tears for a time and place where not to upset her. I was just going to say to my friend that I would love to but this moment was not the right time for me as I was scared and frightened. The door opened and in waltzed one of her friend's.

I could tell from the years of knowing her that she was not happy as this person had been asked to stay away for this hour. She had arranged for this to be my time with her daughter. I did not stay much longer as I found the comments from the visitor to hurtful to stay. I gave my dear friend a hug and arranged to take her and her daughter home from hospital the following day. I would then have time alone with them both then. I walked out of the hospital in a blur; all focus had gone as the tears yet again started to fall down my face. I went straight home and continued to cry for what should have been. What could have been and my own jealousy that all was fine for her so why could it not have been fine for me?

By the time Rosemary called by I had stopped crying and had my strong, 'I can cope' face on and I was trying to focus on the fact I had committed myself to taking them home the following day. I was hoping that I had cried all my tears today and that tomorrow I could be strong and deal with it. I knew that I had still not held her bundle of pink joy. This would have to be something I considered doing tomorrow.

The tomorrows always seemed to come too fast and waking up knowing I was actually going to have to do something I was unsure of, and that scared me; the other side of the coin was that it was an honour to have been asked under the circumstances. It was not the idea of taking my friend and her daughter home, it was more the fact that Heulwen should have been the first baby in my car. If it was not going to be Heulwen then I am glad it was her and her new family.

Collecting her from the hospital was the easy bit. I ended up being able to put a sensible and organising head on. Loading the car with the bags and making sure that she and her daughter were safely strapped into the car and driving them both home was the simple bit. It was when we got to her home and went in to see all the baby things around and the beautiful yellow Moses basket ready and waiting for this beautiful baby that the pull at the heartstrings started. The next hour was a very emotional time for me, my friend went to make a cup of tea for us both and put her daughter in my arms. I did not have a choice; she was in my arms, this beautiful live baby. My friend knew that she was in safe arms, but how could I tell her this was ripping my heart out of my chest? I was trying so hard to not cry. My friend came back with her camera and snapped a picture. The picture if I see it now makes me break as both she and myself can see the pain written all over my face.

Over the few days following being with my friend I felt like I had taken ten paces backwards. I could not get the courage to walk out the front door. Rosemary during this week was my lifeline. How could I explain to anyone that I didn't want to hold her daughter, when actually I did. Though all I really wanted to hold was my own daughter, it was Heulwen I wanted to feed and sing to and watch grow. Rosemary helped me to put my immediate feelings into perspective and at no point was there a negative feeling with the support she was giving me.

Rosemary took her role with me very gently and as the days and weeks progressed I began to truly like and trust Rosemary. In a way it would take sometimes years to develop a lasting friendship. When something of significance was happening Rosemary was much more prominent and she was either there with me or popping round later to be able to talk to.

It was here, weeks after my friend's daughter was born that we had the dreaded appointment with the consultant to discuss the post-mortem results and any questions we had since Heulwen's death. I still had it in my head that I must have been to blame for my daughter's death. This was a time that Rosemary became a constant for me again. She encouraged me to write a list of questions which I had been asking myself over the last seven weeks so that I could go through all the questions with the consultant. She made me talk to Tim as well to identify any questions he may have had. It would save us forgetting anything when the time came. Emotionally the few forward steps I felt I had made over the past weeks were disappearing and I was back to the days when Heulwen died again. I knew nothing could bring her back to me, but something could stop us from trying again. All I wanted was a baby, a family to complete our future life.

The appointment date arrived and we headed off to the hospital where Heulwen died. It was the first time we had returned there since we had left leaving Heulwen behind. The visit on its own was very emotional and churned up many feelings again of blame. Our consultant had arranged for the appointment to be in his office rather than his consultation room. I was so glad of this; how could I have returned to that clinic where there would be loads of happy pregnant women? The fear of the unknown was eating away at my inner soul. The feeling of needing to go and find some answers, coupled with not wanting to go became a torment because I didn't want to hear any bad news.

Our consultant was wonderful, apologising for the untidy filing system he had. Basically he had piles upon piles of patient files on the floor. It was the type of untidy that if someone else came in they would never find anything, but ask the consultant for something and he would put his hands on it immediately. This may sound very silly but it actually helped me to feel more at ease. The clinical feeling was not in this room. Even though we were in the heart of the hospital this room was 'just an office'.

The meeting went really well considering. We were told that Heulwen was a perfect baby, no reason for her to have died. Also that she died of hypoxia. What they also found out was she had a balanced translocation of chromosome 1-21. This was totally baffling to me. Medical jargon and I was lost. He explained what this meant and the fact that she most likely got it from either me or Tim. He was going to refer us to genetics' clinic. They will be able to explain in more details the consequences for us. He also suggested that we do not try for another baby until we have been able to see this person. I was able to also get my list of questions out. He was very positive about this and went through each question with me and explained the answers in a way that I could understand.

The idea of not trying straight away for another baby devastated me. I had to try and stay positive now for the future. My past was so messed emotionally and physically so debilitating I had to find a way to get my head together. It was around this stage that I actually asked Rosemary to call the charity Sands for me. Sands supports bereaved parents and their families through the death of a baby. I had been going to pick up the phone on a few occasions but still unable to actually make that call. Contact was made and they would send an information help pack.

Rosemary had become my confidant, the person who I could discuss Heulwen with and also all my hopes and fears, my dreams and worries. So when Rosemary started to cross the subject of maybe the time had come that a trained counsellor would be a more natural solution to carrying on the grieving process, it was like for a while I was losing the only person who understood me. But it also felt like I had gained a pass in an exam and I was doing alright. Through discussion with Rosemary I realised I wasn't going to lose anything as she would still visit until I was ready to let go and even then she was always a phone call away, just as before. I felt a lot more confident, I had got through the last few weeks and I had survived. I was even thinking about returning to work, though starting back very gently as my job entailed being in the public eye. The seed had been set in my mind that getting back into a regular routine would also be the right progression for me.

My first visit with the counsellor was very difficult. I was again talking to a stranger who was going to help me. She listened, and asked me many times "and how did that make you feel?" By the end of the sessions I know I was feeling so shattered emotionally it was as if I had gone back weeks again. I continued to see her and as time went on she did help me. There is one thing she said that even now sticks in my mind, all those "if only's" change to "I wish". So 'if only I had got to see the doctor when I was in hospital that first time..' to 'I wish I had got to see the doctor when I was in hospital that first time'. It made me think about my feelings and the blame within the grieving process.

We spoke about my intending to go back to work, about those friends who could not speak to me; the reason behind people's ignorance. It always felt to me that because

Heulwen died I was not good enough to be people's friend anymore. In fact this was not true, but how could I say to them 'I understood their reactions toward me' when I was having such problems understanding my own emotions?

On March 25th Tim and I went to my parents', it was their anniversary and we went to celebrate the day with them. This was a turning point for me I was returning to work on the Monday. I was just starting a few hours a day to break myself back in. Just in case it was way too soon I had a get-out clause. So today was the last day that I would be on maternity leave. We had a very relaxing day and just took the time out together. Even though I had been home and we had been together a lot, our grieving had taken different paths and sometimes we were not always together emotionally.

From the last few weeks I could very easily understand how the death of a child could wreck a relationship. We have had to accept each other's grief as well as be a comfort for each other whilst also trying to confront our own needs and emotions. I was lucky as everything was made available to me but for Tim it was much harder. Firstly his masculine pride wouldn't always let him ask for help. Secondly for Tim he was always trying to 'be strong' for me and he ended up doing his grieving in the walls of work. Though it shut me out sometimes it made his life bearable. We always seemed to find comfort together with my parents as they had been the only people to meet Heulwen and for them she was as real as she was to us.

The first day back to work was very draining. Just making the smile stay on my face had been the most tiring thing of all. The day before I had decided it was going to be my turning point. That did not mean I was going to forget my daughter or what had happened, she was always going to be a part of my life. This was the time that I had to look to the future, whether a childless one or whether we were able to have more.

We could not start trying until we had seen the genetic counsellor so I had to put my mind onto something else. I chose to retake my dental nurse exam. I contacted the examining board as it had gone past the last date for applications. They kindly put me onto the cancellation list. I started revising and, with loads of help from my work colleagues I felt more confident about my knowledge. I would still have to deal with my nerves. In any new situations I have had anxiety attacks which debilitated me. So how on earth would I be able to travel to Swansea and then the examination centre, staying calm the whole time? This was something I did not think I could do alone, I needed help.

The exam was scheduled in May 2001. When had been back to work for six weeks. I was still seeing the counsellor but my contact with Rosemary had naturally gone to phone calls whenever I needed her. I felt very comfortable with this because the relationship that had built had grown to a place where I fully trusted her and her ability to be that friend when I needed it. Rosemary now knew things about me that no one else will ever know. The day would come when I would need Rosemary and I knew that when that time came I could just pick up the phone.

It was not until this time that I actually went to the doctor myself and asked for help. I knew that the anxiety would be my failing when I went for this exam. So I spoke to her about the exam and what was required of me to pass. She had just the thing. Something that was a one off that would calm my nerves, enough to be able to drive and sit the four-part exam.

Now this was the goal; I had set my mind on this for Heulwen. Maybe that sounds silly but to me I needed to achieve something within my career as a fulfilment for the motherhood which was still pending. I knew I was a mother, but being a mother with nothing to show was a constant reminder of my inabilities.

I went with a positive mind to the exam. I had to pass this time to prove to myself that I could do it. On finishing the exam I still felt fairly positive. Only two months to wait for the results.

It was the end of May that we managed to get a last minute cancellation to see the geneticist consultant. They had managed to get in touch with us to go. This was actually good for me as I was not able to stew too much on the idea of the appointment. When we went to see the consultant he did explain extremely well with some wonderful drawings; he drew what the translocation meant. I was informed that I was the carrier of the translocation and that we would be highly prone to miscarriages because of it. Having said all that Heulwen and her stillbirth had nothing to do with the translocation so at this stage there is no reason why we can't start trying again. There are ways and means of finding out in later life if any children we had, carry the translocation or not. This must have been the most uplifting news we had had in the last five months. We could try again. I wanted to shout it out loud and dance around (only Tim would have disowned me for embarrassing him). Even though I had the translocation too, it was not a cause or a contributing factor to the death of our daughter.

Our lives began to take on a fairly normal routine. Life for us would never be the same as it had been before Heulwen and we would never be those people we had been then. But the new Tim and Shirley were doing okay. We found that we had become much more sensitive to others while still making a place for our own needs. We tried to spend time together as well as keeping our own hobbies going. I continued to see the counsellor for a few more months, slowly reducing her visits so that when I was confident enough to say I was able to go the rest of the road alone it too was a natural progression.

Each month I was hoping for a positive result on a pregnancy test. In July it seemed to be our month. Sadly at eight weeks

I miscarried. For me that was a strange feeling. Many would have been devastated that again we had 'lost a baby'. I could not feel like that. How could I when it just seemed like a very heavy period with more pain than I normally got. I felt more devastated that two months had been lost on a non-viable pregnancy. My hopes and dreams lay in having a living-breathing baby in my arms.

My relationship with my friend had slowly become very strained and it was now at a stage that we hardly spoke. I did not intentionally want it to become like this but I found myself starting to always see the green eyed monster of jealousy every time I saw her. The time that hurt me the most was totally unintentional on her part. I was having my lunch in a local cafe when she strode in with her daughter in her pram. I could tell she was in a bad mood so I had commented on her obvious mood. She had then responded in an over tired grumpy mood along the lines of 'Well what do you expect I have been up all night with this girl...' The thought nearly bought me to tears at her moodiness and attitude to parenting. My response had been very harsh but honest.

"I would do anything to have the pleasures of sleepless nights with my daughter"

I left quickly after this, though regretting my harsh words in one breathe but also knowing it was exactly how I felt. My friend had not spoken without caring, it was just a normal conversation that you would have had with a friend or another mother. But I was grieving the death of my own daughter who would have been so close to hers in age.

Christmas came and went in quite a blur. We should have been buying toys and presents for Heulwen. All we could do was go to the grave and leave flowers and a candle. I could not find it in me to put up the Christmas decorations this year. It was the first Christmas without our daughter and it was now so close to her first birthday that joyous feelings would not come easily. We stayed home together and had a steak dinner, watched some films, and cried for what should have been.

As the days got closer to Heulwen's birthday we began to both go into our own worlds. Tim buried himself into his work, whereas I did the opposite and booked time off. I just did not know how emotionally we had developed a year on. It was still as vivid as if it were last week. I needed to do something in remembrance of Heulwen and I found this difficult. We both felt that over the last year we had gone to hell and back. How could we find something that would commemorate Heulwen without bringing all the pain and sorrow back with vengeance? We decided to get Heulwen flowers the same as on her funeral day. The teddy bear in white holding two yellow roses seems so appropriate to us both that this is what we did.

My mum and dad came over and put flowers on their granddaughter's grave as well. Throughout the day I was replaying in my head 'what was happening this time one year ago today'. At 11.32 on the 14th January 2002 I cried for all the 'should have been's'. To finish off the day and put the icing on the cake of sorrow, my period started on Heulwen's first birthday too.

I had hoped that I would have been pregnant or even had another baby by the time of Heulwen's first birthday. I began to feel that it just would not be for us. We have had our child and that was it. So quietly I began to just get on with life in whatever way seemed right. I never went out anymore but I did get back into army cadet life which gave me the opportunity to use my instructor skills and work with young people. Their innocence and attitude proved a great benefit to me. It was something I really enjoyed and was able to forget everything whilst I was there because everyone accepted me; the old me as much as the new me. Also I had a wonderful company commander who was very supportive. It also meant I was away quite a bit. It gave me the opportunity to build my own confidence again being without Tim by my side all the time. It also gave Tim the space to get on with his work without worrying about me. This time was good for us as it gave our relationship strength. It helped to know we could cope with day-to-day life but our love for each other was strong and true. It all sounds very soppy, but it was times like this that I knew why I married my best friend.

Chapter 3
Charlie

February 2002

Days and weeks flowed into a month, and when it was close to the end of February without the show of my dreaded monthly I took a home test. It was a positive result, I was pregnant again. Half of me excited the other half thinking if this is yet another non-viable pregnancy then it's another couple of months wasted. I contacted the midwives, mainly to have them available if yet again I miscarried. I would not book in until I had got to the nine-week stage as it would be then I should have a scan. At nine weeks a midwife came round to my home to do the booking in. It was a sensitive time for me emotionally that if I had gone to the hospital for the booking in appointment the whole community would have found out within the day. I was only just coming to terms with my own emotions about being pregnant and I did not want the congratulations yet. Things can still go wrong.

Tim found it very hard to even associate with this pregnancy, and though I understood that it was self-preservation, it did not help me. I was reminded every day that I was carrying a baby in my tummy and I knew that lightning can strike twice. I found it hard to 'attach' myself to the baby inside as I did with Heulwen. Everything was going as expected. I had a different midwife this time. I found it hard to see the midwife I had with Heulwen because of the feeling of de-ja-vu.

I felt more comfortable with the thought of new pregnancy, new midwife. I still had the same consultant as I had never forgotten the promise he gave me. I believed that he would do everything in his power not to let what happened with Heulwen happen again to us. The care I was receiving was wonderful; by the time I was 20 weeks I was seeing consultant and midwife on a fortnightly basis. So I saw someone every week. This I found so reassuring. It was around this time I contacted Rosemary. I just wanted her to know, even though she already knew from the midwives. I felt I was at a stage where things were as positive as they possibly could be.

Rosemary actually came to see me then. For the first time in this pregnancy I was able to talk about how I was feeling. Terrible! I was so scared of history repeating itself that I was struggling to feel for the baby inside, who was now starting to kick me and show a presence. Rosemary was able to reassure me that what I was feeling was a normal experience for someone who had suffered a bereavement. Rosemary wanted to come see me again before this baby arrived, so that I could have someone to talk to. Also there were a lot of feelings and emotions which I would be dealing with and yet again Rosemary would be there to be my confidant.

I was so frightened of not being able to love this baby. We found out at the twenty week scan that I was carrying a boy which in a way I was thankful for. I was worried about not only my own feelings for a girl but also the idea that people would think a girl would be a replacement for Heulwen as that could never be the case. I saw Rosemary about three times prior to our son's expected delivery date. She did discuss with me the possible feelings that could come showing their head once babe was born, and that if I understood the feelings then hopefully it would ease the transition of motherhood and grieving the "what could have been feelings" .

As the months and weeks got closer to the pending arrival the consultant appointments became weekly. All the choices were discussed, and because of Heulwen's size and the obvious size of this babe it was deemed a necessity for me to have an elective caesarean section. The consultant was adamant this was the safest option for babe and me. This time it would be done in a controlled way so that Tim could be present with me and I would be awake to hear that first cry. The date for the c-section was booked. Babe was actually due on Tim and my wedding anniversary on the 23rd of October; the date for the section had been booked for the 14th October. That was the first shocker for me, not only was Heulwen born on the 14th but so our son would be.

I was very frightened of going into hospital and something going wrong, I could not cope with the thought that if all did repeat itself then I did not want Tim to have to face that alone like last time. We asked if my parents would come and be there waiting for us, if something went wrong. Also, they were there for us when Heulwen died so, if all went right, who better to be the first to meet their grandson? What was also very reassuring for me was my community midwife organised a training day at the general district hospital which I was going to be at so that she would be with me in theatre and afterwards on the ward. Even though my nerves by this time were totally shot, I knew that I was going to be well looked after when I went into hospital.

I did feel very inadequate where the preparation was concerned. I had never unpacked my hospital bag after Heulwen. I was unable to emotionally empty it wash, dry and repack it ready for this baby. My mum was my saviour here; she understood me and offered to do the baby bag ready for me. The nursery had not been touched since Heulwen either. I still could not do this. Tim and I talked about this and we decided to leave it until this baby had arrived safely. I knew I would be in hospital for a few days.

So whilst I was going to be in hospital Tim would buy a car seat for this baby, as he wanted to be able to carry babe out in a carry type car seat. As for the sleeping arrangements, we decided that I would make the Moses basket up once I got home from hospital. Nothing would be done until this baby was safely in our arms.

The Wednesday before surgery I went for my last consultant appointment. I remember being very anxious and worried that we were so close now to the date. I was so frightened that we had got so close. Could this actually happen? Could I possibly have a live baby?

I went into the weight and urine check. She said there was a slight trace of protein in the urine but nothing to mark down. This concerned me, because I had heard about protein in the water could be a problem especially with other symptoms like swelling, sickness and headaches. I did say that maybe it was up to the consultant to decide whether it was something to mark down or not. I went through to see the midwife who did the blood pressure check; all seemed normal for me there.

Next stop was to have a sizing scan. They had been doing the sizing scans regularly from 26 weeks, so they could monitor that babe was growing and the placenta and cord did not show any signs of starting to fail as they did with Heulwen. Last stop was in with the consultant. He did his normal thorough checks. I told the consultant about the protein, more to have reassurance that it was fine. He excused himself for a moment to see the lady who did that check.

When he came back to my utter shock he admitted me straight into the ward. He felt he wanted to do a full twenty-four hour protein check and monitor baby regularly to make sure all was alright. I became nervous for being moved into the ward. Poor Tim ended up having to travel home and get a hospital bag for me. He ended up on the road for four hours that day.

It ended up a slow and quiet twenty-four hours. I was hoping desperately that the consultant would just say that they would do the section early. No such luck. After the full twenty-four hours of protein testing and then waiting for the results it wasn't until late the following day that I was able to go home. They wanted me to go onto the ward every day until the day of delivery to monitor baby daily. Even though this would take three hours out of every day, it was fine and very reassuring that they were being very cautious. Only days left.

For three days we travelled to and fro from the hospital for monitoring. I enjoyed listening to the heartbeat, whereas Tim found this noise very disturbing. It was the one thing he was given the responsibility for watching whilst I was being prepared for the emergency section with Heulwen. The noise was haunting him. Even when he knew the noise was for a strong son.

We only had to wait a couple of days now. Would they go quickly enough, would we actually be celebrating in a couple of days? It was so strange a feeling that even getting to this place within the pregnancy I still did not feel I would ever be walking out of the hospital with a living-breathing baby. So close and yet so frightened.

At 6am on Monday 14th October I was awake and having a small breakfast of toast. I then had a long soak in a hot bath. By the time I had relaxed in the bath dried and got dressed I had enough time for a cup of tea before we had to go to the hospital. Neither of us could say those words "this will be the last time there will only be two of us" but we knew it was what we were both thinking. We left our home at 8am. The drive would take about an hour.

On arriving at the hospital we were shown to a bed. We just sat there for a while. I had to have an antibiotic cover at least two hours prior to surgery so the cannula was attached to my hand in preparation for this and the surgery. The room we had been put in was a four-person room. Which was all right and I would not have complained about it. But when they came and asked if I would like to go into a single room I jumped at the prospect. It would save me any embarrassment if I had an emotional moment. My bed was moved into the private room.

My midwife arrived at about eleven o'clock which was great as time seemed to be really dragging now. I was told that I would be the first patient going into theatre as I had a latex allergy. In a funny way this was both good and bad. Good that it would be over sooner rather than later, bad because my nerves were totally shot that I wasn't even sure that I was able to make that walk down the corridor through to the theatre.

Tim and I talked a great deal in these last couple of hours. We had chosen a name for our son 'Charlie' which over the years has been in Tim's family as Charles. I just did not like Charles so we compromised slightly. His middle name would be after his granddad David.

We also spoke of how, with Heulwen, daddy had held her first. I wanted daddy to hold our son first too. It was the only thing that I felt I could control. It was around quarter to two that the midwife said it was time. We had that dreaded walk. I had given her a little outfit for our son to be put into. We walked along the corridor; I had one of those lovely surgical gowns on that leaves a gaping hole down one's back and bum. So to cover my total embarrassment I had a second one on as a dressing gown as well, back to front.

Once we got to the theatre preparation room Tim was taken out to get changed into theatre gowns so that he would be able to be with me. I was given a couple of delightful concoctions from the anaesthetist to hopefully save any sickness and whatever else they do. Trust me they did not taste very appetising. Once Tim was dressed and back by my side we went into the theatre. I was shaking like a leaf in a gale-force wind. I was on the bed ready when the doctor came in. He was a nice man who tried to ease my nerves telling us how he had come off of holiday just for us and that it will be over in no time. Now was the time for the needles; man I do hate needles. I was asked to curl up into the foetal ball. Now that was an experience, how was I going to do this and stay still when I had a huge great big hard lump in front of me? I certainly had a good go. I found it hard to stay still when he was doing the spinal as it was very uncomfortable, so I clenched my teeth and squeezed Tim's hand as hard as I could just so he knew it was giving me some discomfort.

I rolled onto my back and was waiting to go numb. It was a totally weird feeling as I thought I could move and feel but I couldn't. The anaesthetist was pinching me from my toes to my boobs and I could not feel any of it. I did not even know they had started the operation until the doctor said it would now feel like someone was washing up in my belly. It was an odd description, but very accurate.

A matter of seconds after he said that, I heard the sound I had longed to hear for so long. The cry of our newborn baby. My midwife called over after a few moments and said 'you have a perfect baby boy'. I could not hold back the pent up emotion from the last nine months, the tears just started to fall unchecked. Even when my midwife came over and placed Charlie into his daddy's arms I could not really register that that was our living, breathing son, nor could I see him through the blur of the tears.

After I was finished in the theatre I was wheeled out into a bay in the corridor for recovery. I saw Tim wheeling a cot towards us and everyone looking into the cot. It was only then that I asked the nurse who was with me 'Can I see my son, please?' It felt such a stupid question one which I just did not need to ask. She then went and got Charlie for me and placed him on the bed next to me. I looked at this beautiful baby; he had such cute chubby cheeks and was just so perfect. Charlie was laying there as quiet as me we just seemed to be looking at each other. 'Hello sweetie, I am your mummy.'

We went back to the room, me being wheeled on the bed and Tim pushing the empty cot behind us. I could not want to be separated from our special baby. Within a few moments of us being back to the ward room my parents came in. My midwife had gone downstairs to the coffee shop and given them the wonderful news and they came straight up. Charlie went into his granny's arms first; her face was so full of pride and sadness in one. Granddad was next; he was worried about holding Charlie at first as he had hurt his shoulder. But it didn't take a lot of convincing for him to sit down and then have Charlie placed on him for a hold.

Shortly after, the midwife came in to check on Charlie and me. I was really shocked and happy to see the midwife who had been with me when Heulwen was born. It was so nice to see the familiar face at this hospital. She said that she was on day shift so would see me every day whilst I was in. Charlie had weighed in at 10lb 3oz, slightly bigger than his big sister had been. I just could not take my eyes off this little baby boy. So special. My community midwife stayed with us for a good hour after all the excitement and even helped me to establish breast feeding with Charlie.

The rest of the day was full of visitors, Tim's parents came to meet their first grandson and at 9 o'clock Tim was kicked out and told to go home and get some sleep. It had been a long day for both of us.

The night was a long and painful one for me, I was given pain relief. I was constantly looking into the cot next to me. At about midnight the night midwife came in and saw the tears in my eyes. She must have read my file as she came in and spoke with me for a short while, then she placed Charlie in the bed next to me saying to Charlie "I think your mummy needs a cuddle"? I was slightly fearful as I had read that a baby should never sleep in the same bed as parents. The midwife was very reassuring and said she would keep an eye on us. It wasn't long before I fell asleep with Charlie next to me.

The next four days went fairly quickly, I slowly (and with the wonderful help from all the staff at the hospital) started to mend from the surgery. I was back walking about in no time at all and by the Thursday looking forward to returning home. After the initial emotional outburst I was coming to terms with the fact that my son was very much alive and our future as a family was no longer just a dream. Tim was visiting every evening. He was working during the day and saving the time off for when we would be home.

On the Thursday when I was discharged from hospital Tim brought the new car seat with him he had purchased on the way to us. His face was so happy and proud. Our bags were packed ready to go and all was left was to strap Charlie into the car seat and say goodbye to all the lovely staff. I said a special goodbye to our midwife and agreed to keep in touch with her. Tim took the bags out first and then came back for Charlie; it was his thing that he had to be the one to carry his son out to the car. Though it seemed so strange to him to be carrying something so precious, the pride was shining out of every pore in his body.

Our life took on a new role over the next weeks and months. I was very unsure that I was actually doing everything right with Charlie. He always seemed such a hungry baby and I was becoming quite drained myself with the feeding on demand. Rosemary was so wonderful again with me. She reassured and coached for want of a better word. She trusted me to be able to know what was best. Charlie progressed well and it was not long before my confidence built up.

Christmas had a different feel to it this year. We had Charlie with us but we still felt the wrench of loyalty to our daughter. How could we even contemplate enjoying ourselves when Heulwen had been due on Boxing Day? I still felt unable to make a big thing over Christmas so I compromised with myself and put a small tree up. For Heulwen I bought a tree ornament and placed it on the tree to always remind us of her. Not that she would ever be forgotten, but I felt that this ornament can be carried on from year to year and one day Charlie will be able to tell his children about Heulwen's tree ornaments.

Tim and I had never really been the religious type but to us we felt that Charlie was our special child. We talked about having him christened. It was very important to us to make sure that Heulwen was always part of the family. So as close as we could get it to Heulwen's birthday in January, Charlie was christened at the same church as Heulwen rested. My midwife from the main hospital came to his christening and the contact was kept going between us through the weeks and months following Charlie's birth.

Charlie's christening was also another step to building the relationship back with my friend. Now that Charlie was in our lives I felt more able to open myself up to taking time with her daughter.

It did not shock me to much when Charlie was six months old I found out I was pregnant again. I felt slightly more positive about this pregnancy, though still had the small worries that things do not always work out. I tried as I did with Charlie to go into the pregnancy as positively as I could. I was never able to enjoy the pregnancy with Charlie and with Heulwen I was always too sick to enjoy. Hopefully I could try and enjoy this one.

The enjoyment did not last long, as I seemed to have a lot of stresses along the way. We had decided to buy our first home together; up until now we had always rented but Tim had managed to save a good deposit for us to look at an affordable mortgage. We found a house seven miles away from where we lived which would be ideal as a first home. But the stress of buying a new home and being pregnant, and with an eight month old baby, was taking its toll on my sanity.

On top of all the normal stresses. My friend told me she was also expecting a baby. Our expected delivery dates were a week apart. I was over the moon for her and, in a way, this was the thing that brought our friendship back very close. The only thing that now haunted me was a comment I had made to her after Charlie had arrived. I never wanted to be pregnant at the same time as her again. So I had to put the haunting feeling behind me so that we could try and both enjoy these pregnancies.

Rosemary was doing her normal visits and making sure both Charlie and I were doing alright. It seemed that having Charlie was actually helping me as far as the grieving went. I could now speak of Heulwen without crying my eyes out every time. This seemed a very positive step.

Charlie was making wonderful progress to a stage we knew he was a normal little boy. It was strange as it was only now that I was hoping the baby I was carrying was a girl. I could even say I had convinced myself that it was a girl I was having. Again we had regular scans and, though I did not see the midwife as regularly as I did with Charlie, I was left with the open invite to go to clinic or give them a ring if ever I had a worry. I did do this on a few occasions for reassurance if I had not felt 'her' move or it 'just did not feel right'.

My midwife was so very understanding and on occasions just popped in when she was in the area to make sure all was okay. She had been such a big part of my pregnancy with Charlie and already a huge part of this pregnancy that I was quite worried when I knew that she herself would be going on maternity leave before this baby was born.

Through my own selfish worry, I was so happy for her and her family for the pending arrival of their new baby.

My worry was very selfish but who would be there when I had this baby? How would I cope without the face I knew and trusted? I had plenty of time to work this out but it was a constant thought that niggled at me. My midwife's baby was due four weeks before my baby was due. So she was going to be able to see me through until my seventh month of pregnancy.

All was going really well with the pregnancy until around the twenty week mark when we had back the results for the Downs Syndrome testing. We had always said that if the risk was over 1 in a 100 we would leave it and let fate take its course. Only for this pregnancy the risk was below 1 in a 100. So we were given an appointment to see our consultant in the general district hospital to discuss this and make any decisions needed.

We talked about this a lot over the few days before the appointment and had made the decision of having the amniocentesis to identify whether this baby had Downs Syndrome. The silly thing was, I don't think I could have gone for a termination if the result was positive for Downs syndrome. So, for me, having this test was just going to give me time to prepare.

So once we got to the hospital and went in for my appointment we told the consultant our decision. The wonderful thing that happened was he took us straight over to the scanning area and arranged to do the amniocentesis for us straight away: No time for us to worry about it, or to change our minds. The procedure was uncomfortable but bearable. It was the waiting after for the results that was difficult. They had to come from another specialised laboratory.

It was a few days later as we had asked for a speedy reply,

that Tim received a telephone call one evening whilst I was out. It was from the laboratory. They had recognised my name because of Heulwen and wanted to let us know directly firstly about the Downs test which was clear, but to also inform us that the baby had the balanced translocation the same as Heulwen had. She also asked Tim if we wanted to know the sex of the baby.

When I got home Tim was beaming to tell me something. He told me about the Downs result and the balanced translocation. There was still something else. Tim asked me if I wanted to know if this was a boy or girl. I was still very adamant that this must be a girl. Tim said he had found out but would keep it secret if I wanted him to.

"Go on; tell me I can officially buy some pink things again?"

To my utter shock he said to me that I couldn't as the babe was a boy.

Chapter 4
Joe

September 2003

I felt totally heart broken by the news. Not because I didn't want a boy but because I so wanted a girl. I felt that I was ready to have the girl, not to replace Heulwen but to fill the void that her dying had left behind. The news of having a boy actually took me a good few weeks to come to terms with. In a way I was glad to find out because if my bubble had been burst on the day babe was born, would I have been able to bond with 'him'?

It made it hard for me to feel comfortable choosing a name for our new son. When we had found out that we were having a boy with Charlie, it was fairly easy for us to choose a name. We had a couple in our minds and then it just seemed to fit. So, with this babe it was hard. We got down to two names. Harry or Joseph.

Harry, for me this was a name that couldn't really be shortened which is something I do not like myself. Too many people shorten my name to 'Shirl', so you see it has been a pet hate of mine. So Harry I kind of liked. There was only one problem to this; we already had a Charlie. Add a Harry to this and it would feel like all we needed to make the family complete was a William. Royalty we are not. So, Joseph. This name can be shortened to Joe which I could get used to. Could not say I liked the full Joseph, but I could get used to it.

So we stewed on these two names for some weeks and the turning factor was when Tim came home from work and did his normal "how is mummy and Charlie". Then to my swelling stomach "and has 'arry been a good boy today". That very moment I realised that Harry was never going to be my son's name if it could be shortened to 'Arry. So at this point we both agreed that Joe would be our baby boy's name.

The weeks passed slowly with a lot of packing and eventually the move date was set. Three days after Charlie's first birthday we moved into our own home. Many friends helped us out. Mum-in-law had Charlie for the day so we could at least manage to get his cot up and into a bedroom. Even though Charlie had seen the house at this point he didn't understand that it was going to become our home. So when we collected him and bought him 'home' it was a special moment to see, what made it such a memorable moment was when Charlie came in and was put onto the floor to have a crawl about. He did not do as we thought. It was at this moment when he used what furniture we had out to heist himself up and took his first unaided walk across his new living room. Now I knew that this could become our home. It had become special in a matter of moments once Charlie had arrived.

We had sorted a small bedroom out for Charlie. It was going to be a stop gap until I had decorated the room which would eventually be his bedroom. Life seemed to tick along; I went to work which I had only gone back to part-time. I wanted and needed to be with Charlie as much as possible. I felt that I did not want to miss a thing as he was growing up. Tim was working full time, so financially at this stage we could afford it. Charlie seemed to constantly be changing and he always seemed so big for his age as if I was missing something. That was not the case. It was just time was flying by.

It had been decided that I would work until Christmas and

then go on to maternity leave, but this didn't work out. By the end of November I was struggling with my size and severe back ache so it was suggested that I finish work earlier. By mid December I was on maternity leave. It gave me chance to get Christmas planned as Charlie was now more able to enjoy a Christmas. I was actually looking forward to Christmas for the first time since Heulwen had died. I knew that Boxing Day and everyday after that would slowly be a struggle because that was when Heulwen had been due. Though somehow having Charlie there meant we had to try and make the best of what we had and Charlie was that. We felt that we could make this Christmas even more special by making it that family event. Christmas day would always be only us, but Boxing Day we made it extra special and invited both my parents and Tim's parents over for another Christmas dinner. Another being we had all had Christmas dinner on the day and we had another Christmas day on Boxing Day which Charlie loved. He found it hard on the next day because things started to be a bit more normal, except for the fact he had more toys than room.

The four weeks following Christmas I finished decorating Charlie's new bedroom. We decided to move Charlie over into a big bed a couple of weeks before Joe would be born, so that he felt like a big boy rather than he is being moved because Joe needs the cot.

January fourteenth was again a hard and emotional day. Charlie and I took Heulwen some flowers to her grave and I tried to make the occasion something for Charlie to remember; it will always be the little something that we do for his sister. We took pictures and then took them round for Tim to see as he was at work. That night we lit a candle in memory of Heulwen.

Two weeks after Heulwen's second birthday I had the date for Joe to be delivered by elective caesarean section. I had sorted the hospital bags again. Arranged for Charlie to be cared for by Mum and Dad in law for the day. Everything was sorted. Time was getting closer. I had been keeping in touch with the midwife from the hospital who had been there with both Heulwen and Charlie. She had managed to change her shift with her colleague so that she could be in the operating theatre with us. She had become that light for me. It had been a worry to think that all the people in the hospital would be strangers; how could I trust any of them because I didn't know any of them? So all I had to do now was to stay sane enough to get through that day.

Rosemary popped in to see me the week before Joe was due just to make sure I was doing okay, and also to see that Charlie was alright. He seemed very happy with the prospect of a little brother.

The morning came and I felt more nervous than I did with Charlie, though I think the nerves were more from the prospect of leaving Charlie for a few days. I was so frightened that I would not be able to love this new baby in the same way I love my special little boy Charlie. That was scarier than anything. Mum and Dad in law arrived at eight o'clock so that we could leave to drive the hour to the hospital again. I gave Charlie the biggest hug I could muster. My little boy was going to become my big boy after today. So for one last time I hugged him like only a mother can, the special 'mummy loves you always' type hug, and then walked out the door to the car.

The journey was uneventful; we arrived at the hospital and were quickly shown to my bed space. The same as with Charlie happened and I saw the anaesthetist to go over the drugs that would be used for the surgery. We then saw the surgeon. I had asked to be sterilised during this surgery as long as babe was alive and well. The surgeon discussed this with us and made a point of telling Tim that for women the failure rate is 1-100 but for men was 1-1000. So Tim changed his mind and said for me not to have that done; he would be sterilised at a later date. We were told that again I was the first to go to surgery and he would see us later.

My midwife popped in to see us; she was such a good sight for me. I know I could really trust her, which meant so much to me.

The time soon went and I again was in those wonderfully fashionable surgical gowns. Again walking down the corridor, Tim veering off to get into his surgical clothing. Yet again drinking that wonderful concoction. It all seemed too familiar to me. The thought of having the spinal was absolutely petrifying me, because I knew it is so uncomfortable. Tim arrived back at my side in the lovely blue shade surgery clothes and it was now time to go into theatre.

The anaesthetist was now telling me to roll into the foetal position. Tim placed himself right in front of me so all I could see was him. Nice in one respect but also meant he saw every bit of pain that went across my face. I am not sure whether it was my anticipating the pain that seemed to make it worse or the simple fact that I was generally nervous again.

Once again the sensation of going numb was a weird feeling; as it worked its way up my chest it made me feel quite queasy. The anaesthetist immediately put something into my cannula to prevent the sickness as soon as I mentioned the feeling. It didn't seem long before Joseph was born. The much awaited sound wasn't immediately coming. I could feel myself holding my breathe waiting. Then the familiar sound of the first cry came and my breathe came out in a sigh of such relief.

My midwife brought Joseph over for us to see. She said he is a perfectly healthy little boy. She took Joe back over to her area to clean him up and get him dressed. It was now she did the second part of the apgar test on Joe. She came straight over to us and quickly and very calmly said that Joe's scores had gone down slightly and she is going to take Joe over to Special Care Baby Unit to be checked over by the paediatrician just for peace of mind. I trusted her; I had to know she was doing it for Joe. She then said that because of what has happened in the past she wants to be safe. She went holding Joe very close to her chest and took him through to the SCBU.

The team in the theatre continued to finish the surgery and as soon as all was completed I was moved into the recovery corridor. Tim went at this point to see Joe to find out what was happening. Even though I trusted the midwife and her experience, I was feeling totally alone. There was the nurse next to me doing the normal checking of blood pressure and vitals, but at this point I had no son and Tim was taking a lot longer than I thought he should be taking.

Once Tim returned to me it was without Joe, but clutched in his hand was his camera with which he had taken photos of Joe. I needed to see him and was holding the camera as a lifeline to my son. Joe was spread eagled in a cot with a cannula in his tiny arm and a box over his head. He had a nappy on but that was all. I was touching the camera screen as if I was stroking his face. There was warmth there. I just wanted to hold my baby but as I couldn't feel my legs it was a near impossibility to be able to do that.

Tim explained that Joe had what was known as wet lung. Which meant he needed oxygen therapy to help to get the fluid remains out of his lungs. He would only be in there for as long as needed. It settled me down to know that, in fact, Joe was fine and even though he had been gone from me it was alright. It was not like Heulwen.

I was taken back to the ward where two of the other ladies in the ward had their babies with them. This did distress me but I stayed positive and thought only of Joe and knew he would be brought back to me very soon. Once I had been settled back onto the ward Tim and I chatted for some time and soon realised it was getting quite late and nearly time for him to go home. Before he went I had to know about

Joe again; he hadn't even had a feed yet. Surely he must be getting hungry now. Tim, under orders to check on Joe, went back to SCBU to see our son and to take some more photos.

Tim returned with no more news, Joe was still having oxygen and they would bring him back as soon as he was able to come off the treatment. He had used his camera as well as my camera to take photos so left one camera with me and took the other camera home to show everyone photos of Joe. It was about 7pm before Tim left, but I promised to ring him if anything happened. Tim would be back tomorrow with Charlie so I was already looking forward to seeing my big boy.

After Tim left I felt so alone without Joe with me. When my midwife's familiar face poked around the door to see Joe she was quite shocked that he wasn't back by my side by now. Joe was born at 14:52 and it was now gone 19:00. She promised me that before she finished for the night she would find out what was happening.

It felt like forever before my midwife returned, but in fact it was within an hour. She returned with my bundle of joy. Lesley said that she had got permission from the paediatrician for me to see Joe for five minutes but he needed to go back to SCBU as he needed more oxygen.

Five minutes was not enough. She passed Joe to me as at this stage I was unable to do much as I was still slightly uncomfortable from the spinal and surgery. Just to hold Joe was such a special moment; I couldn't take my eyes off him. I tried to feed him but he was not interested. My midwife said he was likely to be very tired from the wet lung. The feeling that he didn't want me was overwhelming but, (for Joe's sake), I had to put it into check and control. So for the last couple of minutes I just looked and stroked Joe's face and told him that Mammy was here and loved him so, so much.

When the moment came that my midwife said she had to take Joe back to SCBU it broke my heart. I loathed to give him away; all I wanted to do was hold him safe in my arms. Reluctantly I gently gave Joe another kiss and passed my baby back to her.

The night was going to be a very long one. I was finding it hard to sleep with others in the room with babies crying and my Joe not there with me. It felt like I was missing an arm. Every time the night midwife came in to see one of the other ladies I asked if there was any news about Joe. The midwife was lovely and kept ringing through to see if there was any change. I tried to sleep and must have got a couple of hours on and off through the night. My mind was constantly on my little man who must be hungry by now.

By five o'clock the midwife said that if I managed to get out of bed and hold down some breakfast she would take me to see Joe. This was an offer I could not refuse. I knew it certainly would be a challenge. I still had a catheter in and I hurt but a bit of pain was not going to stop me seeing my son. The midwife could see my determination and first lifted the head of the bed up so that I was in a more sitting position. Then I swung my legs round; the sweat from the challenge was building up on my forehead. Slowly I shifted my bum to the edge of the bed and connected feet with floor.

I was braced myself for the pain. I held my tummy and the midwife supported me whilst I lifted myself up into a standing position. Only four steps needed to get to the chair, I could do it. Shuffling very carefully I moved myself over to the chair and slowly lowered myself into the seat. First part achieved, half way to seeing my little Joey. Now food, I couldn't wait; I knew that would not be a problem. I have always loved my food and at this moment was absolutely starved. The midwife bought some toast with marmalade and a cup of tea. The tea went down so quickly. It is amazing how the water that is always available never seems to fill the same spot that a nice cup of tea does. All the toast soon disappeared the same way the tea went. That was it, I could now go and see my Joey.

True to her word, the midwife returned pushing a wheelchair. What I must say about this lovely lady is she was not a spring chicken, she was a more mature lady and very petite with it. Now me, I am no lightweight. So to keep her word to me could not have been an easy feat.

With her support again I got into a standing position, with a bit of a shuffle I moved myself over to the wheel chair and sat down. Now I covered myself waist down with a blanket whilst the catheter bag was attached to the wheelchair. We were ready to move. She wheeled me through to SCBU. Code doors stopped every passage. I wasn't sure whether I was going into a prison or coming out of one. It all seemed to take so long, but it was worth the wait.

I was pushed into a room with about ten cots in. A nurse was in the room going around the cots. I heard the midwife say 'Baby Gittoes' and this is where the most stupid of sentences came out of my mouth "I'm his Mammy ". This did bring a small giggle to the dark room. The nurse replied with a smirk in her voice "I kind of worked that out dressed like that." Obviously I was in my nightdress and dressing gown; gave it away really. Looking at the row of cots I felt so inadequate as unless she had pointed us in the right direction, I had no idea which baby was Joe. I could not see him for looking. As soon as I looked into the cot I saw my beautiful son and realised I would have recognised him even if I had had to go from cot to cot.

This was the first time that I spent with Joe undisturbed. The midwife left me there and said she would come back and get me in a while. I had time to really spend with Joe. The room was in half light as it was still very early and the nurse who was in the room sensed I needed time and carried on with what she was doing within the room, just for a short while. I just stared at my Joey, he seemed so relaxed with his eyes wide open. I stroked his face and forehead which he seemed to love as he seemed to move into the feeling. I couldn't just sit there watching anymore. He was attached to what seemed to be loads of wires which made me frightened of hurting him. The nurse came over and explained what everything was for, the pulse and oxygen saturation levels.

I wanted to hold Joe and the need was so great. I asked the nurse if it was alright. She helped to get Joey out of the cot and placed him in my waiting arms. I felt so comfortable with Joe in my arms. He was a lot more alert now compared to the night before and when offered the chance to feed his appetite, he didn't take long to latch on. I spent about an hour with Joe and after the very restless and nervous night I was finding it very hard to actually stay awake. All the pent up emotion and fear of having Joe taken away from me when he was delivered had quietly taken its toll on me and seeing Joe now made me realise that the midwife was right and just being protective.

As I was about to be led away from Joe by the lovely night midwife, Joe was placed back into his little cot where the machine continued to bleep for his oxygen saturations. They were nice and high which was what the doctors were watching for. Joe was going to be just fine and back with me in no time. Over the next two hours I spent a bit of time by my bed. I knew from experience with Charlie that I had at least two hours before I needed to worry about Joe needing another feed. Now that I had seen Joe and felt confident that he was going to be fine I spent the time wisely and sat down for a while, had a shower and just generally relaxed as best I could. I was very sore and knew when it was time to have some more pain relief. I was unsure of what to do at around eleven o'clock when I wanted and needed to go back to see Joe. I now felt a lot more refreshed than I had earlier and wasn't sure if the walk was a wise move for me so soon after surgery. I asked one of the midwives who said if I took it very slowly then I could walk. If at any point I felt unwell or faint to call for a staff member.

I didn't need any persuasion and slowly walked the distance to the SCBU where the staff in there were taking great care of my son. I sat with Joey for as many hours as I was allowed. Charlie came to visit both me and his brother and when he had got to the ward and found us not there Tim knew exactly where I would be. When Charlie came in he was suddenly my big man at fifteen months. I got my little hug from Charlie and then with some trepidation he took his first look at his brother. He was unsure of the wires but once we explained that it was fine he stuck his little hand into the cot to hold his brother for the first time. I took the photo as Tim held Charlie up to peer into the cot.

I spent as much time as I could with Joe in SCBU over the next two days whilst he was in their care. On Wednesday Joey was brought back to me on the ward. The feeling of having him actually next to me on the ward was wonderful. Joey still had a cannula in his little arm and this worried me intensely. I was frightened in case I would hurt him when I held him, how do you change the clothes on him whilst he had this 'thing' in his arm. This was all revealed to me when the ward 'mum' came round and so wonderfully showed me how to bathe, dress and generally love Joe. For some reason it all felt so new again. Even though Charlie was still so young, Joe was totally different and suddenly he had different needs. Having said that I also knew once the cannula was removed Joe would be a normal little baby just like I had had with Charlie.

The following day Joe had the cannula removed and the final checks required from the doctors and he and I were discharged from hospital. Tim came to pick us up and arrived at about 4.30 p.m. To my utter amazement Tim then told me of his ordeal to even get to the hospital. It had rained so much that there was a lot of flooding. The main roads that would get us to and from home were all closed due to the floods. This was quite a shock as I really had not realised it had been raining so much, let alone enough to close the roads.

I had already packed our bags so everything was ready to go down to the car. Tim took the cases down to the car and then came back for his family, Charlie, Joseph and myself. We said our goodbyes to the wonderful staff and got to the car. The journey home was longer than normal because of all the diversions but it was a lovely feeling that our family was now complete and this perfect complete family is home.

The next two days we spend precious time getting to know Joseph and giving Charlie loads of big brother loving. We saw a midwife every day not only to check on Joseph's progress but also to check on my wound. At this stage I was healing very nicely being six days post operative. Joseph had settled into breast feeding quite well and fed every two hours like clockwork. He had even settled into going about four hours at night time which at less than a week old I was over the moon about.

On Sunday we had a lot of visitors coming and going and Joey didn't seem to feed as well, but due to all the company and cuddles he was getting I was not unduly surprised. It wasn't until the midwife came at 6o'clock that I realised Joseph had not had a feed since noon. Neither did he want one either. I had offered but there was no interest. The midwife checked Joey over to make sure he was not obviously ill, but she seemed quite happy and agreed with us that he had been overly fussed; we were to monitor him and if we became concerned to telephone the doctor.

The midwife left shortly after and I sat just cuddling Joey in my arms, willing him to root for a feed. It was when I was sat with him that I noticed he was twitching quite violently with his arms for a week old baby. I called to Tim who was in the kitchen with Charlie, to come in and have a look.

I felt concerned about this and so did Tim, mainly because we had not noticed it before. So what we decided to do was to ring the midwife first and get her advice; seemed sensible at the time. The midwife felt that to be safe and err on the side of caution we should contact the on-call doctor.

I continued to hold and comfort Joe whilst Tim was waiting on the telephone to speak to a nurse, who would then arrange for the doctor to ring back.

As every minute passed Joseph seemed to be deteriorating, the jerking spells seemed to be increasing and lasting for longer. I remember thinking with all my first aid training I was watching my son and felt helpless. Just before the doctor rang back I said to Tim, "If I didn't know better I would say he was having a seizure".

The doctor's call was short and basically we were advised to go to the local community hospital 'now' and he would see Joseph straight away.

Tim held Joe whilst I whizzed around and got a nappy bag together for both Charlie and Joseph. Then coats on and into the car.

The car we had at that time did not have a light in the back. I was so worried about Joe and felt his breathing was becoming very raspy. I would not be able to see him if he was in his car seat, so I got into the back of the car strapped in and held Joseph so close to my ear that I was able to hear his breathing, just so that I knew he was still alive. It was only now that I realised there was something really wrong with Joseph. Tim secured Charlie into his seat and then drove as quickly and safely as he could to the cottage hospital where the doctor was waiting.

Tim pulled the car right up to the entrance and helped Joseph and me out then he got Charlie out and we all went inside. We were ushered into the waiting room and seemed to be there for ages though it was probably only minutes. All the time Joseph was going in and out of the jerking spasm. When the doctor eventually called us in I am sure I seemed and looked like a wreck. He asked that I put Joseph onto the bed and for me to sit on the other side of the bed to keep him comforted. He was looking Joseph over when another jerking session started. The doctor spoke very quietly but with urgency to the nurse who got oxygen for Joseph and held the mask over his face. He then quietly said to me that Joseph was having a seizure and he was going to arrange an ambulance to transport him straight to the main hospital where he could be better cared for. Tim was to follow in the car with Charlie.

Once Joe had come out of that round of seizures the doctor went straight to the telephone and arrange urgent transportation to the general district hospital where Joseph had been born. Tim stayed for as long as he could but as it was a Sunday evening and he knew the car needed petrol before the garage closed, he said he would join us at the hospital.

Just as Tim was about to leave an ambulance pulled up outside and a very familiar face came through the door. It was a paramedic, who was also my first aid trainer and a special friend. He was also the first responder called in for Joe because the ambulance that would be taking us to the hospital was still fifteen minutes away. The doctor asked him what needles he had as they had nothing small enough for Joseph there. The ambulance did not have a needle small enough either. The doctor then decided that oxygen therapy would be enough to get to the hospital rather than putting Joseph through extra stress at this stage when the main hospital would have everything that would be needed.

I remember looking at the paramedic and wishing for a miracle. I remember saying "I would like to introduce my son Joseph". How silly those words seemed. He could tell that this was my Joseph, he only had to look in my tear-stained eyes to know. I knew that the quiet tears were falling down my face; I could not stop them, just thinking about how serious Joseph's condition was. I needed to be strong for Charlie and Tim when they met up with us at the hospital.

When the second ambulance arrived we were ushered in. I sat up on the stretcher bed with one strap across my legs. The one he wanted to put across my stomach hurt my wound to much so he left that off. Then I held Joseph in my arms. The paramedic sat on a seat next to us watching Joe closely. The doctor gave the paramedic the information that he needed and my paramedic friend gave me a reassuring nod telling his colleague jokingly to "look after this one!"

The journey started at a normal pace with the paramedic chatting a nice calming conversation whilst constantly watching Joseph. When Joseph had a seizure he quickly and calmly placed the oxygen mask over Joe's tiny face until he stopped. Then he put the mask down, slid his seat up to the driver and then wheeled his seat back to my side.

He said that he had asked the driver to put the blue lights on and to continue without stopping but at a normal speed. He felt that with the blues on it would mean that our journey would be quicker getting Joseph in to the hands and equipment of the hospital. This seemed very logical to me, though slightly worrying. I knew that Joe was being looked after.

It only seemed a few minutes after that conversation when Joseph had another seizure. Again the paramedic placed the oxygen mask over Joe's face and monitored until the seizure stopped. Again he then slid his seat toward the driver and spoke quietly, then wheeled his seat back to our side. Before he had chance to tell me what was happening I felt the ambulance accelerate quickly. He explained that he would be happier getting Joseph to the hospital in the quickest and safest manner. So he had now asked the driver to drive on full blues. This meant that they would, if safe to do so, go though red lights and pick the speed up. I remember that at this stage the journey in a backward position was making me feel travel sick so with all my strength I concentrated on Joe and tried to ignore the journey except the blue light reflection that was shining through the darkened window.

It did not seem long before the journey came to an end and we arrived outside the hospital. I was expecting to get off the bed to walk in but was informed that I was to stay put as it was policy and hold Joseph whilst they took us both up to the children's ward, where we were expected. We were wheeled into a small side ward where Tim and Charlie were waiting for us. Tim took hold of Joseph whilst I got off the wheeled stretcher. I listened as the paramedic went to the staff that were sitting at the desk and explained all the details and included the seizures during the journey.

We continued to wait in the room for what seemed like ages. Joe had another seizure and I looked at Tim with tears streaming down my face. I did not want to say too much as Charlie was in the room with us and I really did not want to upset him unnecessarily. Still the staff did not come in. Then Joe went into another seizure and I could feel Tim getting frustrated. Tim walked out to the desk quite calmly for his inner mood and told the staff that it was happening again.

The senior staff nurse walked in and looked at Joe, who was now in my arms. He took Joe straight out of my arms and placed him into the cot bed that was in the room. Within moments Joe was stripped down to his nappy and had an oxygen mask on.

Also two other members of staff had joined the team. So Joe now had a doctor and two nurses with him.

Time at this point was totally irrelevant. I could not tell you what time it was or how long I had been standing there just watching what was happening. I was frightened to leave the room in case something happened, but knew that I had to go to the toilet it was only down the corridor so I quickly left Tim in the room whilst I nipped down to the ladies. I was as quick as I could be, and returned to the room.

I got to the door where only moments ago I had left Joe and Tim they were not there. I could not see any of the staff that only a few minutes ago had been here with my son. It was only seconds but felt like minutes of sheer terror before Tim appeared behind me. They had moved Joe into the high dependency room where all the extra equipment was available. Tim took me into the room where I saw Joe in a small clear cot.

The cot was just above waist height to be easier for people to work on. Joe was connected to monitors again and already a cannula was connected in his tiny little hand. I knew it was very late and long past Charlie's bedtime by now. It was now that the one nurse and the auxiliary nurse started to discuss possible options for sleeping. They had rooms available for parents staying with their poorly children and one of the rooms had a double sofa bed. We decided that Tim and I would do a shift basis so that one of us was always with Joe and the other with Charlie. We both went to the room first to settle Charlie down to sleep, and through sheer exhaustion, I had forty winks with him. I was only asleep for about an hour as the sleep that came had been too restless. I waited for Tim to return, which was not that long, and then I went back to be with Joe.

The staff were still working on him and next to him constantly. I was able to sit next to his cot and just watch occasionally touching his hand without interfering with what they were doing. Time again passed in a daze and I remember the staff saying that they had contacted the consultant on call to come in but they were still waiting.

I found myself watching the monitors, believing that they were keeping Joe alive. I was too frightened to watch Joe though the need through the fear was so strong. I knew Joe was a very poorly little boy, I could see with my own eyes that he was still having the seizures, and to me they seemed to be getting more frequent now than they had been before I had taken Charlie to bed.

For the first time in many years I sat there watching my son, praying for a miracle. It seemed that a miracle was not going to happen. Without any obvious fear I watched as the staff nurse started to do chest compressions on my little boy. I was rooted to the spot as I heard him tell his colleague to call the crash team. Automatically and without realising I had done it I had moved myself to the one wall away from Joe so that everyone that needed to be close to him could get in without me to hinder them.

I could not leave him now; my back was to the wall, the tears running silently down my face. This can not happen, I thought I can not cope if another of my children dies.

The consultant walked in at this moment and went straight to Joe's side. Still I could not leave, I kept hearing myself say "I wasn't there for Heulwen; I have to stay for Joe. Whatever happens I needed to stay".

The nurse came over to me, I expected her to ask me to leave in a manner that held no choice. She didn't and when I said I had to stay I felt she understood. She asked if we should call Tim. If something went wrong and Joe died whilst Tim wasn't there I knew that he would always feel guilty. Though I also had concerns about Charlie being left alone, in the room. I had need not have worried as the auxiliary nurse sat with Charlie so that Tim would be able to be at Joe's side with me.

Tim came to the door of Joe's room and halted, he saw what was happening and he just broke. His face went as white as a sheet and his eyes looked at me with sheer terror. I was being torn between my husband and my son. My need to stay with my son in case something happened and knowing my husband needed me by his side. I had to think who needed me most. The staff was there, and they were looking after Joe and doing everything within their power to save him.

I walked from the room just as the crash team were entering and I sat in the room next door to Joe holding Tim and praying for that miracle to happen. We sure could do with a miracle to save our son.

Tim had always been the stronger person emotionally but for the first time through all of the troubles in our joint life the roles had suddenly reversed. For me this was a coping mechanism. Taking the role of the strong one saved me from breaking apart inside. My heart was breaking in pieces; my son was fighting for his life. My husband was breaking apart at the seams and I was trying with all my strength to will my son to keep fighting.

We could hear the mumbles of the conversations in Joe's room; we knew that it was medical talk as the words that did drift through were all to do with what they were doing to Joe. I remember trying to listen and then trying to shut them out as I was scared about how much they were hurting Joe.

It felt like ages that we sat in the adjoining room not knowing what was happening though I am certain it was less that an hour. When the nurse eventually came in to us. Her face looked grim and I was so fearful of bad news that I was frightened to ask. I didn't need to ask as she soon said "You have a very poorly little man in there but he is breathing unassisted at the moment."

She informed us that Joe had arrested but he had stabilised without the need of assistance through medical intervention. The need to see Joe for myself was strong and Tim felt the same as his hand was squeezing mine that little bit stronger. I tentatively walked into the room Joe was in and felt Tim very close behind me. When I looked at Joe I wanted to scream out and sob. His little chest was all bruised from the compressions they had had to do on him. The nurse and doctor were still very close to Joe and monitoring all that was happening to him. I felt unsure about going to Joe, frightened that my presence would hurt him I was even more frightened of him dying.

We were reassured that it was alright to touch Joe and hold his hand. No more encouragement was needed. I just leaned on the side of his crib and held his hand. I stayed there for what seemed like an eternity. I needed to be there, I needed to stay and remember everything. Not let a single memory go unchecked. How could I cope if Joe died, I could not even think about it but it kept popping into my mind. It was obvious at this point that Tim would find the prospect absolutely unbearable. How could we both hold ourselves together?

Once we had spent some time with Joe and settled our thoughts together again the doctor came to see us. The news was very grim. They told us that Joe was extremely poorly and at the moment they were trying to just control the seizures but as yet this was proving to be difficult. They were not optimistic about Joe even coming through the next 24 hours and suggested that we contact the immediate family to warn them in case they wanted to come and see him. I had not realised how the time had moved on as, to my surprise it was 5am. We decided that I would make the phone calls and Tim would stay with Charlie so that when he woke up one of us would be with him. Tim felt that he was not in the right mind to call anyone so it was left to me.

I stayed with Joe until 7am and then I knew my dad would be up so felt it was a good time to start the phone calls. The staff were so lovely and took me to a quiet office so that

I had privacy to ring. I was left alone with a box of tissues and the phone.

I rang my dad first; I knew that I could draw the strength I needed to keep going from his voice alone. Something over the years I have found hard to do is ask for 'help'. He was firstly very shocked to hear me on the phone so early in the morning but from my voice instantly knew that there was something wrong. I explained what had happened during the last 12 hours and what the doctors had said about his prognosis. I also had to ask dad if anybody on our side of the family had ever had seizure, specifically childhood seizures. To dad's knowledge there was only my uncle who had seizures which started as an adult. I took all the information down ready to tell the consultant. I chatted with my dad for a short while longer continually drawing on his inner strength whilst knowing he was only holding onto it for my sake.

My next call was to my mum-in-law. This call was a lot harder, knowing how emotional my mum-in-law can get and with her the emotion is of an inner type; she closes in and immediately puts the wall around herself. I had to sound very strong and controlled on the phone to her. At no point could I let her know just how much Tim had broken down or how close I was to breaking. So again I told Mum everything that had happened, leaving out any part which I knew would overly stress her at this point. There would be plenty of time later to fill in the gaps. Again I asked the question about whether there was a history of childhood seizures within the family. Mum could not think of any at this point so after saying my goodbyes and promising to keep them up to date I went with all the information back to Joe's bedside.

Watching Joe laying very still, totally dependant on the tubes and wires connected to him broke my heart even more. Joe had now gone nearly 24 hours without a feed of any kind. I was aware that now one of the drips Joe was receiving was a saline drip to prevent dehydration. That did not help the mother's instinct to want to feed her baby. I had started to express my milk so that when Joe was ready to feed then there was my milk ready in case for any reason I was not available.

I sat and just prayed for a miracle. I did not know who I was praying to; I could not to this day answer that question. I knew that whoever could hear me would do something to save my baby; protect him from all the pain he must be suffering.

Joe was in the high dependency unit so there was always a nurse with him so my prayers were silent, but continuous.

It wasn't too much later before Charlie was up and about. The biggest problem we had with respect to Charlie was the lack of nappies. I had only put into the car my normal carry bag which had two of each nappies. We had long used them. The staff again came up trumps for Charlie and found suitable nappies for him.

So once he was clean and back into his clothes Tim and I took turns on being with Joe and then spending time with Charlie.

Emotionally I found this so difficult; I was battling demons in my head which were telling me that my need to be with Joe at this point was greater than my need to be with Charlie not that I didn't love Charlie greatly. If something was going to happen to Joe I had to be there. I had always felt I had let Heulwen down by not being awake and with her in her last moment, although deep down I knew I must have been. So the over powering feeling now was that if I was there and conscious of everything that was happening then he would never be alone. So my visits to the playroom with Charlie were enough for him to understand that I loved him and cared about him, but the need to return to his brother was so great I could not deny myself that. We could not tell

Charlie how serious Joe's condition was. We felt that he was too young at this stage to understand the implications of 'very poorly'. So when we said very poorly he seemed to accept that with a light hearted youthful expression.

At a more reasonable time in the morning (about 8.45am) it was time to make some more phone calls. This time to my best friend, who was due within the next two weeks and to Tim's work place.

I decided to go outside and make the calls from my mobile, getting some fresh air in the process. Tim did not feel able to make any calls. The first person I called was my friend; the conversation that had been haunting me over the last couple of hours was the time I said to Clare that I never wanted to be pregnant at the same time as her again. After Heulwen and her daughter were so close and our friendship had taken such a beating I couldn't do that again. So now years on from that, we were going through this turmoil and she was also pregnant. Would life repeat itself and my friend have a lovely healthy child and our precious son would end up with his sister?

When I got hold of her, I explained all that had happened all that the consultants had said. I cried on the phone to the special friend I had here and again prayed silently that Joe would be OK so that she and I would not end up having more pressures on our friendship. After quite a long chat we ended the call with me promising to keep her up to date and she saying she could be at the hospital within the hour if I needed her at all. Though deep down I was unsure whether I could have put that pressure on her, being so close to her own due date.

I then called Tim's work place, explained what was happening and asked them to field any customers and calls for Tim, which they were only too willing to help with. Again I had to promise to keep them informed of Joe's progress which at this point for me was basically asking me to let them know when he died. It seemed like platitudes to me. How could anyone understand what I was watching our son go through? How my dear husband was breaking and I just didn't know how to fix it for him.

It was still fairly early in the morning but it felt so late in the day as neither myself nor Tim had got much sleep to speak of. Charlie was probably the only one who slept in this little adventure.

On my way back to the ward I popped into the hospital shop for some basic personal care products as neither of us had clean clothes or wash bag. I was now out of nappies for Charlie and was hoping to buy some in the shop but was disappointed as there was only new baby size available. I also got a few snack bites so that I had something in my bag for Charlie and Tim to eat.

I took the lift back up to the top floor with a slowness to my step. I was frightened of what the next 24 hours was going to bring, I knew that I was scared to the extreme of Joe dying. How could we cope with that strain on our relationship? When Heulwen died we were lucky that our friendship as well as love got us through it. To consider going through a similar ordeal again was just to hard for me to even contemplate.

The short walk to the ward entrance seemed to only take seconds where in fact I had wanted it to take a good ten minutes so that I would be able to compose myself again before I had to try and put the happy face on for Charlie. I really didn't want him to take on too many of our adult worries until such time as we had no choice.

I returned to the room Joe was in and sat by him. Tim was in the room and Charlie was quietly driving a car up and down the corridor. We waited and watched for a long time. I know for myself, time was irrelevant as there was nothing that either one of us could actually do but neither of us felt able to leave for any length of time. We took turns to spend time with Charlie and play with him. When the play room was open with a play worker in there they kindly watched Charlie. In that room as well so many other workers within the hospital tried hard to make the ordeal as bearable as possible for Charlie.

During the course of the morning a new paediatrician introduced himself to us. Unknown to me he had already met Joe when he was in the SCBU only eight days previous. He explained to us the tests that they intended doing on Joe during the day and also he explained what they all meant. They also intended doing a lumbar puncher test on Joe to rule out meningitis. Dr M (as we fondly now call him in our home) was a very patient gentleman who was so kind to this paranoid mother. He drew me pictures to explain what was happening. This was a great help as I felt as if all control was being taken away from me yet again where my son was concerned. I needed to feel like I had some control in understanding if nothing else.

Joe so bravely went through all the tests. The only thing I was unable to actually watch, though I did from a guarded place behind the window, was the lumbar puncher. It was during Dr M's visit with Joe that yet again they had to use another drug to try and stop the seizures and I realised this patient man was also very willing and able to 'get his hands dirty'. Joe was not always that receptive to taking the drug and when a drug was inserted anally Joe promptly let off wind which shot the drug capsule out. Dr M being on hand in the right place did what was necessary to get the drug into Joe's system. Still being able to have a kind comment about Joe even in this very dire state.

Joe continued to have tests including an EEG. Drugs where constantly being introduced to control the seizures and Joe fought on to stay with us. It was whilst I watched Joe in this cot fighting for his life that I knew from this point on he would never be called Joey by me. He had to much fight in him to hold a pet name of such softness. So from that moment on I called Joseph either by his full name or shortened to Joe.

Tim and I continued to take shifts with Joe and Charlie throughout the day with both being available when Dr M came in to see Joe.

At about lunchtime on this first full day of Joe being in hospital there was a phone call through to the ward. A staff member came to get me and asked me if I wanted to talk to Rosemary. Straight away I knew it wasn't just Tim and me anymore. I spoke to Rosemary and during the call I also gave permission to the staff to keep Rosemary up to date with Joe's progress. If or when anything happened I felt that I would need Rosemary close by.

Through the conversation and explanations I also spoke to Rosemary about Tim and the way he was at this stage totally snapping at the seams. It was worrying me nearly as much as Joe's condition itself. Rosemary was able to then prepare herself. I felt I was splitting myself in half trying to stay the supportive partner in the relationship whilst also trying to care for and love my son for whatever time I had with him. It was taking its toll on me. Rosemary was my sanity, the one person who at this very moment in time I could openly state my worst fears both about Joe and his prognosis at this point and also about Tim and the effect this was having on him and our relationship. I was frightened of so many things and still trying to keep the strong brave face on for the people who needed that right now.

I had no idea how Rosemary had found out Joe was in hospital so quickly but I am so glad she did as I knew that just the short conversation I had with her helped me to hold myself together that little bit longer. The called ended with Rosemary promising to ring through to the hospital the following day and if I needed her at anytime before then to ring through, she would make herself available if needed. Just knowing that was such a relief; the knowledge was enough to keep me going until the next call from Rosemary.

By late afternoon Tim and I had to make some decisions on the sleeping arrangements. I felt that staying another night for Charlie was a very bad idea as he was getting bored and fed up in the hospital. Being of such a young age it was difficult on him. We all were in need of a bath and change of clothes. So logic said that one of us needed to go home with Charlie and to bring supplies of clothing and wash gear the following day for the one in the hospital. The obvious choice for the one to stay was me as I was breast feeding and I did want to be available if Joe ever needed me. I was still expressing milk but this was something I felt I needed to do. The other and more practical reason for me to stay being I was unable to drive at this point after the surgery only a week previous.

So at about 4.30pm Tim left with Charlie to go home and get both himself and Charlie fed. I promised to keep him up to date on any changes in Joe's condition. It was a very tearful 'see you tomorrow' we shared. I was torn between Charlie and Joe and vice versa for Tim. Also Tim had no idea what he would be facing the following day when he returned; 18 hours would be a long time.

Joe was still very much fighting and every now and then I got an open eye looking at me whilst I sat next to him just stroking his face, forehead and hands, whatever I could just touch and remember for the rest of my life if that was what was going to be.

It was during this quiet time I had with Joe that something unique happened. The staff were having their changeover so I was with Joe alone. The room Joe was in had been lacking outside light for most of the day as the window in the room looked into a courtyard of which all four sides was hospital. So the sun would have great difficulty shining into this room.

I sat quietly stroking Joe's forehead, tears running down my cheeks as I prayed with everything I had. This time it was not to a god or any of the unproven religious icons. This time I prayed to Heulwen. I prayed to her to ask her to watch over her little brother, asked her to be there for him if this was his time. Ultimately I asked and prayed that she would save him so he could stay with us as the pain of losing one child was unbearable but to have two children die did not bear thinking about. By the time I had finished my prayer to my daughter I was a blubbering heap, but felt I was unable to do any more for my son other than be there for him.

Now this is where I open my soul up as something so strange and only really significant to me happened. The sun shone. The sun shone through the window; it wasn't like a sudden blazing sunshine it was like a small ray shone through the window and landed on the foot of Joe's cot. I remembered it and gave myself a little joke saying that at least Heulwen heard me, though didn't let anything else come of it. Deep down I knew that Joe's condition was very serious and even though he had continued to fight through the day at this point there was not much improvement in his condition. He was still not feeding and receiving fluids only intravenously. Drugs where still being pumped into him to try and stabilise the seizures. So the sunshine was dismissed from my mind as quickly as the thought had come into it.

It wasn't long before the night staff came in and said hello again. It was the same staff as last night when we first arrived by ambulance, so we were familiar with each other. The head nurse asked if I had got any sleep during the day, but to be fair it was plainly obvious that sleep was the last thing on my mind at this present point in time. I popped into the kitchen now to make myself a cup of tea. I felt able to do this when someone was in the room with Joe.

It was when I came back into the room that Joe had his eyes open again. They seemed so dark looking at me but sure enough they were both open and looking directly in my direction. I went back into the chair which had been my perch for the day and again softly spoke to Joe and continued to stroke his forehead. I felt that he actually liked this feeling as the way he responded seemed very positive. It felt as if he moved his head into my fingers or thumb when I stroked him. For the next hour Joe seemed to stay fairly alert to his surroundings and to me with his eyes open continuously. This seemed to me such a positive thing but still I was too scared to really think positive; frightened of the possible knock down to earth if it all went wrong.

It was after this long spell of Joe being alert that the nurse suggested if I would like to try and feed Joe it could be a positive step for him. This was not something I needed to be asked twice so kindly the nurse (being male) left the room and the female nurse remained to help get Joe out of the cot. It worried me all the wires and tubes going to Joe. Naively I thought that some would be disconnected but obviously none of the equipment could be disconnected at this time as it continued to monitor Joe and remained the early warning for the medical personnel looking after him.

So attentively I held Joe in my arms and offered him some breast milk. I was surprised how quickly he fed and how hungry he seemed. This made me feel very reassured until the nurse stuck his head round the door and said not to let him feed for too long as he was still very poorly and feeding will sap a lot of his energy. He needed that to carry on fighting. It brought me back down to earth with a bump. I knew they were doing everything for Joe. There had been discussions early about moving Joe to Birmingham Children's Hospital but Joe's condition was too dire to risk this. So I let Joe have a feed from the one breast, had a cuddle and let him then return to the safety of his cot and the staff. It wasn't long before Joe dozed calmly off to sleep. A normal fed and watered baby having a nap this thrilled me to a point of believing there was hope.

It was getting late and I felt that this was something that would cheer Tim up before he went to bed. So I went into the ward reception and rung through to Tim. I told him of the development that had happened this evening and how Joe had stayed alert for some time and also that he had fed. Also I told Tim about my prayer to our daughter and the sunshine and the slight improvement in Joe's condition. I knew at this point I was clutching at straws but these particular straws seemed nice ones to me.

It was much later, or perhaps even the early hours of the following day, that the nurse suggested I went and got my head down for a while. He promised that if anything happened they would come and get me. So with this reassurance and the fact it wasn't really a request, I took myself off to bed. It was quite amazing how emotions had carried me through the last 48 hours. I was exhausted, and in pain myself from the section which in reality was only eight days ago. Sleep was a blessing.

I was woken very gently about six hours later by the student night nurse. I immediately started to worry until she said "don't panic but your son is rooting to be fed". What a feeling that gave me! One he was still alive, and, two he was looking to be fed. I quickly got myself decent and went down to Joe's room. I sat on 'my' seat and fed my beautiful brave son again. This time I fed for a little bit longer than the night before whilst still being conscious of the demands feeding would have on his little body. I felt that if it was little and often this would be better at this stage for him than over doing it so that he became too weak to keep fighting his battle for life.

I was beginning to feel more able to get myself a cup of tea, or a bite to eat, without taking away my presence from Joe now. I was being fed with the hospital menu as I was breast feeding so I was not going hungry. Now I was able to physically eat the food being given to me as I had a reason to keep the breast milk supply. Joe needed me to be strong too.

Rosemary rung the ward before Tim had arrived on the Wednesday. The staff gave Rosemary an update on Joe's condition and then I was able to talk to her for a while. I found that our relationship as health visitor and client had changed at this point to much more. Rosemary was my friend and confident right now. I needed to chat with her even if it was just to be able to remain sane in this very unpredictable world. We discussed the improvements in Joe's condition, and also how I was feeling. The call again ended with the knowledge that, if needed, Rosemary would come to the hospital and was certainly at the end of the phone. Again, she would ring the hospital the following day.

Tim arrived with Charlie just before lunch time. Both were washed and clean and smelling so nice. Charlie had to have loads of cuddles as I had missed him. Tim had also bought a holdall with some changes of clothes, wash kit and one of my huge bath towels. That was so inviting that I went and spent time on me. I spent time on the shower paying special attention to the section scar area which seemed a bit troublesome. After the long soak down in the shower I was able to get some clean fresh clothes on. It felt like heaven.

I managed to get some more surgical pads from the ward to cover the scar to aid healing as I realised that the previous 72 hours had not done me any favours with healing and taking care of myself. I made a mental note to get in touch with my midwife as soon as I got home to check everything out for me. I would mention to Rosemary when I spoke to her next. She may have a suggestion in the meantime.

It must have been nearly an hour before I returned to the ward and Joe, but the hour had been well spent and well needed.

The remainder of the day continued along a similar path as the previous day. Dr M had popped in to see Joe and was positive about the fact he was now feeding reminding me to do little and often so as not to overdo Joe too soon. Though the improvement with Joe overnight was obvious, he was still not out of the woods. They still needed to find the drug which would control his seizures.

I went and had a nap whilst Tim was there and I took Charlie with me to try and keep his routine as normal as possible. So, Charlie and I had an hour's sleep while Tim spent time sitting next to Joe.

Tonight Tim left at about 5pm and took Charlie for food on the way home. I was fearful of the change of routine in Charlie's life as he had been on his own for fifteen months to now be bombarded with a little brother who was in hospital with our focus more on Joe than on Charlie and his every day life. I suggested to Tim that Charlie bring something with him the next day that he and I could do together whilst Tim spent time with Joe. I gave Charlie a big mummy cuddle before they left. I still needed to see and feel Charlie. More so now, if truth be known as I feared losing everything that meant anything to me.

I spent the rest of the evening by Joe's side talking to both Joe and the night staff who again were the same team except for one. I felt I enjoyed the nights more than the days as the day time was very busy. Tests were done, staff were busy and the hustle and bustle of a busy children's ward was very evident. By the evening and night time all the day surgeries had gone home which only left a few night case children in and the few emergency cases with parents worried and bringing their children in to be checked. So I was able to have a conversation a laugh and joke. A small amount of outside life or the edges of a realisation that the world is still moving, and people are continuing with every day life, oblivious to the fact that so many people and babies where fighting for their lives as Joe had for the last 3 or 4 days.

Again I left Joe's room about midnight to get some sleep. I knew that I would fall asleep quickly as I was so totally emotionally drained and exhausted. I was sound asleep as soon as my head hit the pillow. I was able to sleep until I was woken by the student nurse because Joe was rooting to be fed. The staff had tried to keep him going as long as they could with the use of a pacifier but the stage had come when even that was not working. So I got myself decent and went and fed Joe.

Today was Thursday and was the first day that I could actually acknowledge the day. We had been here since Monday with Joe. Today was a more positive day for Joe as his condition was improving all the time. The consultants felt that they had found a medication which Joe was responding well to. This was such a step forward. To see Joe go from nearly continuous seizures, to now being able to stay alert and watch and with sounds express himself. This was such a beautiful thing to see and hear. I understood how poorly Joe had been and there were many unanswered questions still remaining. But there was now hope that we may have the time to find the answers, where as just forty eight hours ago Joe's condition was critical and time was very limited.

On Friday, after the consultant had done his rounds and seen Joe's continued progress, it was suggested that Joe could be moved out of high dependency to room number 2. This was a very scary prospect for me as it was a room that a) I could sleep in with Joe, and b) the medical equipment was not as extreme as the room next door the high dependency.

The move was very quick and, though daunting, I found that I actually loved this time. I had a lot of quiet. With only two machines connected to Joe there was little noise coming from them. So at long last with Joe less than two weeks old I felt that we had some quality time together. I sang to him, told him all about his daddy, his sister and his big brother. It wasn't unusual for people to hear my mumblings to Joe. Joe seemed very content listening to his mother's voice. I noticed during this special time with Joe that he was a very quiet and contented little baby. When he wanted food was the only time that he made anything resembling noise.

Over the next two days I had to learn all about Joe's medications. At this point he seemed to be on many, one to reduce the swelling on his brain, one to control the seizures and another antibiotic. The thought that I would have to be able to understand all of this and then administer these drugs to Joe did frighten me. I had to fight just as Joe did with his life. I had to learn to be strong too.

On Saturday 14th February, Valentines Day, Joe and I stayed in hospital without a visit from daddy. Sadly Charlie had picked up a bug and was unable to make the hour's journey to the hospital. Joe was my little valentine that day. We continued to converse in our own little language, Joe gurgling in answer to all my twittering.

On Sunday when the consultant came round on his morning visits he told us that all they were waiting for now was for Joe to have another EEG. This meant we could be in the ward for over a week whilst they waited for the appointment. The hospital was concerned about the possible travel implications it would cause if they sent Joe home at this point and we just came in for the EEG.

I was unable to drive for six weeks after the surgery of which I still had another four weeks to go. I knew this could be a problem but I also knew that with all the family we have around us someone would bring us into the hospital for an appointment for Joe. I felt that our staying in hospital would only agitate me as I was still missing Charlie and was concerned that he was poorly at home and mummy wasn't there to look after him.

It was decided that Joe was going to be discharged home and we would return for his EEG on notification via phone or letter. The nurses were wonderful, they went over all the drugs again just to make sure I was certain of the doses and they made sure that we had at least a four week supply of the drugs. Tim came alone to the hospital to collect us and take us home. Charlie was still very unwell so was being looked after by Nana. Tim was looking totally drained and I was concerned about Charlie as well as trying to take on board what had happened to Joe over the first two weeks of his life.

I was so glad to be going home, not only for myself but because I felt that Joe would be able to settle more into a routine at home. His medication had to be given every twelve hours and in the hospital this was not a problem as the nursing staff gave it all to him at 2am and 2pm. With medical support I had to change the times for Joe's medications. It wasn't possible to change in one step to 8am and 8pm. We had to adjust it slowly, 30 minutes at a time. Just to get the medication to more social hours it took over a month. Every day seemed to go in a haze for me.

We got home from the hospital. Tim stayed home for as long as he could going to work for a few hours each day for the first week before going back full time. Once Tim was back to work it was up to me to look after Charlie and care for Joe. Joe's seizures had to be counted on a daily basis. Also they had to be timed. His medication had to be measured exactly and given at the correct times every day. Joe didn't like the taste of the phenobarbitone and it broke my heart having to force this medication down the throat of my baby. I found many ways of doing this which made the ordeal as easy as possible for both of us.

Rosemary came to visit within days of us returning home from the hospital. I found that the support I had from her during this period in my life was the most valued to me. She became more than my confidant. I spoke of my concerns about Tim and my feelings and inability to care properly for Charlie. I felt I was only just surviving myself. It was so hard for me to accept that not only had we been cursed to have had our daughter die, we also had to go through a life of uncertainty.

A life there did not seem a future to when my son was having between 80 -100 seizures a day. I couldn't keep count, I know I was supposed to. I knew that he needed me to, but as I counted I had to time them too. I lost count so frequently. It made me feel inadequate as a mother. All I had wanted was a healthy child. A child who could have so many things in life and become anything he wanted to become. How could I look to a future of such uncertainty as this? My son was damaged goods. It had to have been my fault. No one else could have been able to do such damage. It had to be me that was cursed. It was like my son had died too, but he was still here. Not the son I had dreamed of, but a shell of the perfect child we should have had.

I would never have said any of these things to Tim. As his response at the time would have been along the lines of "don't be silly" or "there is nothing wrong with Joe, it will work out". I wasn't in the right place to believe any of it. It would be 'Tim just trying to make me feel better'.

Rosemary came and visited regularly. Sometimes just to pop in for a cuppa. I knew she was working but it felt like she was being the special friend who I could really talk to, she cared.

Three weeks after Joe was born, my friend delivered a healthy, beautiful baby boy. The baby yet again I just craved for. How could I speak to her about my feelings? She had two beautiful healthy children, whereas I had a dead daughter, a son who was even at 16 months becoming my helper, and young carer for his little brother, and Joe who had a future of such uncertainty, living with seizures. At this point we could only imagine what other damage has been done because of the time in hospital and the continued seizures.

Daily life seemed to just pass in a routine of medications and recording. Hospital appointments came in the post thick and fast. The EEG appointment came through when Joe was about four weeks old. Once I was able to drive again (which was around four weeks after Joe was delivered) I was able to take him myself to the majority of the appointments. However with the EEG appointment I was not so comfortable going on my own. It was more because I was unsure of what would happen. Whilst he had been in hospital they just did the test whilst he was in the crib.

Tim and Charlie came with me and Joe for this appointment. We had the hour's drive again to get to the hospital which did not feel as emotional as it had been three weeks ago. We went to the department and I was comforted by the familiar face of the sonographer who had done the same tests on Joe previously. I was still breast feeding Joe, so when we were invited into the room where the test would be done I sat on a nice comfortable arm chair with Joe on my lap. Joe was very restless when the wires were being attached to his head and I ended up feeding him whilst this was being done. Thankfully Tim and Charlie had gone off for a walk which meant it was very private with just the three of us.

I found it made the whole procedure a lot less stressful on us all. It all took about an hour and a half in total, which was not as long as I had thought it would be. The whole event had not been that daunting after all. We were told that the results would be available for the consultant within the week and I would hear from him directly. At this point that seemed fine with me as I knew that Dr M would be seeing Joe in the local clinic during the next month as it had already been pre-booked.

After the appointment we popped into the town to get Charlie a treat as he had been so helpful to his Mummy. So a small car toy was his chosen treat.

Everyday life was becoming quite draining for me. I ended up blaming my hormones, and the stress of Joe's medical issues. I found it difficult to count the seizures as I found myself questioning if they actually were seizures. Or was it my paranoid mind playing tricks on me? No one else seemed to feel the jerks Joe was having was anything other than normal baby movements. It made me question my ability to be Joe's mother. Was I cut out to do this? My sleep was becoming more and more erratic. This was only made worse by the four hourly feeds for Joe. I found myself only half sleeping as I needed to keep reassuring myself that Joe was still breathing, that the monitor was working correctly.

I no longer had midwifery care and physically was healing extremely well. My main connection with the outside world was with Rosemary. She visited every week with additional visits if she felt the need.

I knew I was struggling on an everyday basis, though understanding why was not coming easy to me. I could not identify why I felt I had lost control. I spoke frequently to Rosemary just to try and have the view and opinion of someone else someone who could look at my life without the emotional baggage that went with it. Rosemary was always a great insight for me; she looked at life so openly that it was a breath of fresh air. I was never frightened of confiding in her. This included my personal thoughts about my inadequate ability to care for my son.

We spoke frequently and Rosemary discussed how I felt after Heulwen had died. Why would Heulwen's death be clouding my caring abilities for Joe? I could not understand. Joe was alive and strong which I was so thankful for. I know he wasn't the healthy child which, as parents, we all wish for, that would be something that over time I would have to come to terms with.

When Rosemary suggested I see the counsellor again I did not question her or her knowledge and experience. She knew probably better than me what would be best for me. So I agreed and left Rosemary to arrange an appointment for me. I knew that Rosemary would not do anything without having discussed it with me first. She only had my best interests at heart.

Joe was a very quiet and placid baby. I never knew whether this was because of the medication, or because he was a very contented baby. He would feed and sleep and happily coo at me from his bouncy chair as long as I was close by him. Compared to Charlie, Joe was the complete opposite. I was always trying to please and include Charlie in the everyday life. I felt constantly that I was neglecting him. He was still a baby himself and my attention was diverted by Joe's existence and condition.

Charlie took to the big brother role with interest. He would help me get the nappies and enjoyed being able to be 'big'. He loved the photos and I felt I was always snapping the pictures. Charlie would always try and play with his brother, even though Joe was too small to reciprocate the games. Charlie's laugh when he managed to get a giggle or smile from Joe filled the home with such joy. It was the only sound which melted my heart and let the emotions drain for the very short period.

Chapter 5
The Journey

September 2004

Six months passed very quickly and I seemed quite oblivious to the time scale. Joe was still having daily seizures and they were still averaging between forty and eighty a day. I was getting more knowledgeable about the medications and understanding the ratio of body weight and medication. Dr M was very much a common name in our home as when Joe's weight went up I was either contacting Dr M by telephone or arranging an appointment. It was at Joe's appointment with Dr M when he was seven months that we discussed changing the medication Joe was taking.

It was a very daunting prospect of changing something which I had only just got used to, only just started to make Joe take without him spitting it out due to the foul taste.

It would be a slow changeover; I would have to keep Joe on the phenobarbitone until the new medication was at a sustainable level for the seizures and then slowly reduce it. This process was going to take some weeks to get to the final goal of Joe being on the one medication which should be better for his age. It would also mean I would have to be very organised. By now I was actually getting very good at the medications and recording of his seizures.

The changes in Joe were very slow at first, though still quite obvious. His seizures started to reduce within a very short time of taking a low dose of the new drug. By the time we got to taking the full dose of the Sodium Valproate Joe was actually having seizure-free days. By the time Joe was completely off the phenobarbitone he had managed to have a full week seizure-free. This was something I actually found hard to deal with.

It suddenly occurred to me how I had missed my baby's first 8 months of life. I was so engrossed in the everyday medical needs of my son that the needs of the mother had been put to one side. The feelings crept up on me so slowly that, until they were on me, I didn't realise how much I had held it back. Now I was feeling alone and grief stricken. Grieving for the loss of so many things. First my dear daughter Heulwen. Then it was the health of my son Joseph, and now I had lost without realising the first and most precious months of his life. The only good unaffected thing that I had done in my life was my beautiful special son Charlie, though now at two years old he had to learn to be a young carer.

Rosemary was the only person who I could really talk to about my emotional state. When I spoke to Tim he really could not put himself in a place to understand. He was just grateful that as a family we had got through this. The question was, had we got through it? Was I doing okay? I felt like I had been holding everyone together for so long and now that everyone seemed together, was it ok for me to fall apart?

Rosemary helped me put life back into perspective again. Yes, I am grateful that my dear miracle son is alive and still with us. The realisation that I may very well be able to go back to work at the end of my maternity leave was now looking like a possibility rather than a distant dream as our son was going to need my constant 24/7 care. All these things seemed to contribute to an emotional state of uncertainty and to a point of feeling Joe doesn't need me anymore.

Being able to talk through the last ten months with Rosemary made me in my own mind realise my own inner issues. We would not have survived if Joe had died too.

Joe was nearly eleven months old and doing quite well. He had the occasional seizure but they were down to his weight going up and the medication not sustaining him seizure free. They at worst would be about 3 a day during the 'down hill slide' period. Once his medication was adjusted back up he was good again.

The New Year saw me going back to work. I started back doing the full three days a week as I was prior to going on maternity leave. Joe and Charlie went to a child care nursery just up the road from work. I felt extremely nervous leaving Joe with anyone. It was hard for people to recognise his seizures and I was not truly sure that the childminders understood the importance of recording and recognising Joe's seizures.

Even though I was back to work, Joe still had to see Dr M the consultant on a regular basis. He was still in overall charge of the medication increases. It wasn't until Joe was eighteen months that I was allowed to change Joe's medication dose. So on many an occasion I had to take time off work for these appointments. Joe was also a lot more susceptible to the bugs that every child shared around schools and nurseries, one of the many difficulties I had with work. I found I was becoming an unreliable employee. Prior to the birth of Joe, I had prided myself on being reliable. Everything had changed since then. After twelve months of being back in work I handed my notice in to my boss. I knew that if it had carried on as it was she would have had to reconsidered my employment status. I knew I would not have liked to leave this job with any bad feeling as it probably was the best job I had ever had.

How I got involved with Sands. This is probably a story in itself but it happened so positively that I have enjoyed the journey and found a new passion in my life where Heulwen could still be a part of my family unit.

It was during the Christmas period of 2004, when through the 'grapevine' I heard someone in the small town where I live had just lost their baby daughter who had been born stillborn. This news seemed to really knock me. When Heulwen had died I had been told it had not happened in the area for nearly eight years previously. Now four years on another family had been broken and devastated just like myself and Tim. How I wished I could help in some small way, just so this family knew they were not alone, just so they realised it wasn't only them. I left my phone number with a couple of friends just to say if the bereaved mum wanted to talk to someone then I was around.

It was on Heulwen's 4th birthday anniversary 2005 when the phone rang. When I answered it there was a quiet voice on the end of the phone. How the voice just bought back so many memories. The pain emanated down the phone. This call for me was the start of what my future was going to become. This lady at the end of this line was going to become a special friend. We spoke for nearly an hour with the promise that I would call and see her later that week. I wanted to make a difference to someone else. I had got through all the things in my life because someone took time to hold my hand. Someone to walk the rocky path with me. Now, I wanted to walk the rocky road with someone else.

Within the week I went and visited the young mum. I looked at everything she had of her daughter. I was introduced to another angel. A beautiful princess was in the photos. Perfection in every way. She asked me about Heulwen and how I felt at the time. This made her emotions seem normal as if I had just given her permission to grieve. Everything Rosemary had said to me all those years ago when Heulwen died all came back. I realised that, for this lady, I had walked the same emotional and tragic path she was now walking, and that I had also felt what she was feeling now; this gave some control back into her own shattered life.

I had always known I wanted to do something to help support others through the death of a baby, though I never actually knew what would be my ability. I was in the process of arranging small fundraisers for Sands. Now I just knew what I needed to do. What I could do? I knew that just being there had already helped this young mum. I wanted to be able to help everyone. I remember Tim (always the worrier) telling me to take time and take it slowly. Not to bite off more than I could chew.

I got in touch with Sands again. This time not for my own support, but to find out what I could do to help. It was the opening conversation I needed. I was given clear ways to start. What I could do? How I could help? This was it, I now knew what I wanted to do! What I needed to do to help my life be complete in the sense of having all my three children around me, whether it be in body or mind.

The steps from this were slow but certain. Fundraisers were arranged; I felt that making people aware of a charity which nobody really knew anything about was important. It is like many charities out there; if you have never been affected you are not aware of the charities offering support. This is the same for Sands, though it was amazing how many people came to us whilst doing fundraising events to just say, "My mum had a stillbirth" or "my son died stillborn twenty years ago". This gave us all a sense that we were doing the right thing for all these people who were coming forward to say hello and how they had been affected.

For twelve months we worked on setting up a Sands support group in our quiet rural area, which had seen in the last twelve months, another two stillbirths/neonatal deaths; more families affected, more families suffering. In February 2006 was the opening of our local Sands Support Group.

Rosemary continued to be my constant support, though the support had shifted from the bereaved parent to the working mum who continued to watch over her sons.

Joe was two and actually doing well. He had just started to walk before the Christmas and was exploring his new abilities. Charlie was continuing to develop well. Rosemary had become my professional friend, encouraging me where the Sands charity was concerned and supporting me as my health visitor where my children were concerned.

It was in early 2008 when Rosemary contacted me to let me know of some changes within the health visiting sector and how this was going to affect me. She knew that after seven years of trusting and building this relationship how it would affect me. Suddenly I was going to have a new health visitor. I knew that another twelve months and I would not require a health visitor anyway as the care would go over to the school nurse. It was a weird feeling that I felt people who I did not know were making choices for me without even discussing them with me. I still saw the health visitor due to having to have Joe weighed so regularly with regard to his medication. I felt cheated out of the twelve months. I was so glad that Rosemary had made the point of explaining the changes to me. I knew then that even though the professional connection had been severed the friend who I had learnt to trust and respect would always be there.

As the Sands branch continued my relationships with medical professionals grew at a local level. I was constantly in contact with the head of midwifery who was always supporting the Sands branch. She was always promoting midwifery training in the area of bereavement. It was in 2008 that the local health board and our local branch of Sands decided to do a joint training day. The conference included two workshops. The first workshop would be the co author of the Sands Guidelines for professionals, which had been released a few months previously. The second workshop was to be on continued care and how the professional could continue the support for the bereaved family. It was felt that the positive life that I had led due to the ongoing support which Rosemary had given was a great example.

So I asked Rosemary if she would join me to deliver 'our' story. I will never forget what Rosemary said to me when I had asked. She always said that it was part of her job, though I knew from my time with other bereaved families, that my health visitor did so much more.

The conference was an eye opener for both of us. There was a mixture of medical professionals and bereaved parents there. I started to tell my side of my life. Rosemary joining in either when I got choked up and unable to speak or as and when a professional viewpoint was required. I spoke of Heulwen, Charlie and Joe. The ups and downs of the death of one child the joys of another. The constant need for some kind of normality. Also the value of the continuity of care especially on the long term level. Finally how the care which I had received had secured my 'good health'.

It was at this point in my life I knew I was where I wanted to be. I can hold my head up high and tell people the 'I had made it through'.

I knew that life would throw many obstacles at me. Joe and his care will always keep me on my toes, and in the two years since that conference in 2008 much has happened. Joe and Charlie are both in school, achieving the best that each of them are capable of. Joe is getting some great support within the school and though we have had some ups and downs with his education and medical conditions he amazes me constantly for he is such a happy child.

I still continue doing whatever I can for Sands, and will continue to until no one ever needs the support from a charity dedicated to stillbirth and neonatal death.

Rosemary and I have continued to work together on a voluntary basis which included us having the privilege of speaking together at another conference in London.

I would like to think that by writing this book together, telling our story, (which I am certain would have had a different outcome if Rosemary had not been my health visitor) we will give others a chance to explore how they can make a difference.

Book Two

Chapter 1
Introductions

In health visiting, the antenatal period is an important time. This is because on the one hand it allows communication to take place between midwifery colleagues in terms of notification of a pregnancy. It is also a time when the health visitor can arrange a home-visit to introduce herself to a mother to be and go through the role of the health visitor and discuss what they as heath visitors actually do. However the most important ingredient of the antenatal visit is the opportunity to start a relationship that will go on for a very long time. I always think that the ante-natal visit is so valuable as once the baby is born, the last thing a new and tired mother needs is a stranger called a health visitor standing on her doorstep.

A midwife had told me that Shirley was expecting a baby. As the time drew near for me to plan a home visit, I was also mentor to a health-visiting student. Health visiting students carry a small caseload to enable them to get some experience prior to final exams. Their practice is carefully monitored. It was my student health visitor, who visited Shirley ante-natally and I understand the visit went well. She was a kind and caring person who enjoyed contact with our clients and was well on the way to becoming an excellent health visitor. We then waited to be informed of the birth.

A later telephone call from a midwife informed me of the tragedy. I had few details to work with only that a stillbirth had occurred and that Shirley would be coming back to the local Cottage Hospital maternity unit to be nearer home. I remember that a midwife met Shirley on the hospital doorstep. It was much later that midwife told me that she and Shirley cried together, upstairs in the maternity suite.

My midwifery colleagues looked after and supported Shirley in the days after she returned home. The quality of care they gave was exceptional and spent a lot of time with Shirley while keeping me informed. They gently let Shirley know that I was also standing by to see her when she felt the time was right and in return I was able to gage when I should make contact with Shirley. As the midwives withdrew, I arranged to call and see Shirley. I then began an internal wrestling match that all health visitors go through when a bereavement visit is pending. These are the times that a professional training does not prepare you for and years of experience does not give you all the answers either. The question I kept asking myself was, --'how do you help someone with a broken heart?' — the answer was, and still is, I don't know.

The front door opened and standing in front of me was a person totally enveloped and consumed by grief. The 'come in and sit down' was an automatic response. My 'I'm so sorry to hear the news' felt both inadequate and useless.

I think words at this time have to be carefully considered as a thoughtless remark can stay with someone for the rest of their lives. 'What should I say?' is often asked by professionals, the best answer I can give is -- *nothing*, while that takes courage, *being there* for someone in an honest and caring way is far more valuable than you can ever believe at that awful time. Sometimes it must also be accepted that a grieving person will not be able to cope with a health visitor visit at that time. That should never be taken personally or considered to be an indication that that person is coping, has the help and support required or excuse to never try and visit again. I have heard grief described as feeling like an intense burning, a totally consuming unbearable fire. How can anyone feeling so desolate be in a position to be able to respond as we as professionals think they should to an offer of a visit? Some people will be able to cope with an offered visit early in their grief, some later and some never. The implications of all these three are greatly important when considering future long-term care.

Shirley and I found ourselves sitting on the sofa in the sitting room. No words at that time would be any use or comfort. My professional training, all the books I had read offered nothing at that point, but 'shall I put the kettle on?' and holding Shirley's hand, did. I have to admit that my instincts took over at that point; we health visitors are supposed to be good at that. Mine have served me well over all the years and they are always something I take notice of. We are (and need to remember that we are) human too and our humanity can often lead the way, if we are prepared to listen. Sometimes the professional 'tag' gets in the way. Professionals need to be in touch with their empathic and common sense side as well as their professional, egotistical, detached and afraid-of-litigation side. This means that within certain boundaries, health visitors should be prepared to go that extra mile to deliver a supportive care that is useful to families who are experiencing grief.

The visit was a long one, the story traumatic for both of us, a story that had to be told over and over again during the next many months. It should be remembered at this point that a couple coming home after such a traumatic event still have to face more agony and anguish because of, what professionals call, 'the practical issues'. Shirley and Tim (not forgetting the grandparents) had to cope with a post mortem, register a death, arrange a funeral, support each other through a tidal wave of grief and emotions and come home to an empty void.

Shirley would be producing milk, another reminder she would find difficult to deal with. And never forget the preparations, toys, clothes, the nursery at home waiting for an infant that will never come. All these things and related agony Shirley and Tim had to live with every second of every day. There are no textbooks or guidelines that show parents how to deal with such a situation, just emptiness and despair. How should they react, how do they approach people, how will people approach them, will they ever smile or be able to laugh again? Some comment or words can feel like a knife stabbing at the heart. Shopping becomes a nightmare, confidence drops like a stone, guilt sits on a shoulder ready to give a reminder that a baby wasn't brought home everything becomes slow motion. Colours may remind parents of a little girl lost to them, the radio, TV, hopes and expectations all ready to remind parents of the agony they try to carry deep inside them.

This has nothing to do with deteriorating mental health: It is about being human. So it is very understandable that I can get very angry when health visitors consider they have no place or services to offer to families that suffer a stillbirth. I find that attitude short sighted and very worrying. It must always be remembered that such a traumatic situation, if badly handled or not handled at all, will remain a primary and agonising trauma for the rest of that mother and father's life. In all it's a life sentence, whether other children come along later or not. All these things I was aware of as I sat and listened to Shirley's pain, a pain that you can almost touch.

Shirley felt she would like me to call again I felt strongly that I must be led by her. Weekly visits became the norm with daily visits when needed. Shirley would ring me if I was needed. It was nothing to respond to a telephone call immediately or clear my diary for a morning or an afternoon to be with Shirley. As it became possible, Shirley talked about the things she felt she needed to explore. I wanted her to feel safe with me and that whatever she said, shouted, cried about or cursed about I would never break her confidence and that whatever she said was OK.

Chapter 2
Grief and Pain

As the weeks went by Shirley and I seemed to develop a relationship that was useful to her. She talked about the birth of her baby and covered the event in minute detail. I was introduced to Heulwen and we talked about a little girl who was real and who would be part of Shirley and Tim's family forever. Through the weeks I watched Shirley agonise about her pregnancy and delivery. I saw disbelief, physical and mental pain that was overwhelming and frightening. Shirley through all of this voiced her concerns about Tim and how he was grieving differently to her. We had many conversations about how she might support Tim and help him. Many times I offered to talk to Tim. Shirley felt she could use what we talked about in a positive way to help Tim but the offer stayed open for Tim to pick up if he ever wanted to.

This really highlighted an important area that should never be ignored. The loss of an infant involves two parents. Both will need support and care. And never forget the extended family. Each individual experiencing grief, probably in different ways. Agonising what best to do, -- speak about it, --- never mention the bereavement, -- 'least said sooner mended'. It should not be too surprising that families that are so vulnerable at this time can bruise and damage themselves, sometimes irreparably. But in truth each is often trying to do the 'right thing'.

Another area that generated extreme pain is the response of friends and neighbours. Again people wonder,' what do you say or do?' The result can be situations that cause crippling agony to the bereaved parents. Friends stop calling, cross the road as the couple go down the street. In their fear of 'what to say', may make statements like 'never mind you will have another', when perhaps 'we are here for you if you need us' would be enough.

'Getting back to normal', whatever that means produces it's own hurdles. Shirley was very unsettled and felt very unsafe when Tim went back to work. That in itself should not be trivialised. Facing work and workmates and getting back into a work routine must have been very hard. It is often said that 'time is all it takes', that is partly true but it was quite a parcel of time before Shirley began to feel secure at home, alone with all the memories and nightmares. Time on your hands does not always help good healing,(everyone heals differently).

As Shirley and I got to know each other quite well, I felt she was beginning to trust and feel safe with me. Grief is like an onion. With every layer peeled, more pain is released. We only ever went at Shirley's pace trying to deal with each block of anguish, the depression, guilt, sadness and tears. Emotions are devastatingly powerful and can change at a moment's notice. It is so important that information about a grieving process is given quietly and when appropriate as so many while totally enveloped in darkness feel they are going mad. It is appropriate to reassure someone that the stages of grief are **normal** *while keeping an eye out for the symptoms that can creep in that might suggest what is actually being experienced is not.* Poor care will worsen a situation and families' distress; the effects of this can be long lasting.

Shirley experienced most of what grief can deliver. Loss of sleep, seeing and hearing an infant, guilt, disbelief, constantly rewinding what had happened, trying to help

Tim, coupled with the realisation that dreams would be unfulfilled and plans made would never come to fruition. And, of course the helplessness. Cruse, a charity that supports the bereaved, states that how you respond to a bereaved person will be very individual and personal. Grieving is different for everyone and there is no right or wrong way to do it. If the proper care is not given at this time some individuals will grieve and experience pain for the rest of their lives.

There will always be a time when life presents a situation that is nothing short of being an emotional mountain. That occurred when Shirley's friend delivered her baby and Shirley decided to visit her in hospital. We had talked about this pending situation, initially Shirley's feelings about the pregnancy. Feelings that were so strong they took Shirley by surprise had the potential to become destructive and use up a phenomenal amount of energy. Part of facing those emotions was to recognise and actually acknowledge them. There was a point that I was able to say what Shirley was thinking and how her feelings were exhausting her but that what she was feeling about a pregnancy and subsequent birth was understandable and did not make her a bad person, just a person in pain.

Shirley did go and see her friend and new baby; it was so hard for her. The situation did not go quite as planned and many tears followed. I had arranged to visit Shirley at home after she had seen her friend. I think by the time I arrived on the doorstep it would be fair to say Shirley was 'toughing it out' to say the least so it was important that we gently talked about her visit, her feelings and that empty chasm that had swamped her. Shirley and Tim are not short of courage and true to her type Shirley had offered to take her friend and baby home from hospital the next day. I'm sure that day took many deep breaths from Shirley and a firm control of her emotions.

It was certainly a time when I was available to Shirley

whenever she felt swamped or desperate by situations. That takes a lot of time, but I would always say to colleagues and managers that it is time well spent. A person's future that has become so fragile needs careful, consistent support and perhaps health professional need to be aware that the ability to share energy to support another is not a detrimental thing. Some just call it empathy.

Shirley and Tim still had to go through a meeting with her consultant where 'reasons' for Heulwen's loss would be given. Sadly it doesn't always work out that way and 'reasons why', if any, don't often give the solution or relief that is longed for. A *no reason* can be overshadowed by a giant *'why?'*

As I was very conscious of this, and because of the trust Shirley had shown me, we talked about seeking some specialist advice in relation to her grieving process. Shirley agreed and I asked a colleague who was a Community Psychiatric Nurse to see Shirley to be sure all the care possible would be given to her and to guide me in case I could improve on my approach and care. Shirley had some sessions with the CPN, and had a great benefit from doing so. I continued my visits and availability to Shirley.

Chapter 3
Moving Forward

I had a few times mentioned to Shirley that there was an association called Sands that was supportive to grieving parents. I had never pressurised Shirley to look into this as she was in no fit state to pick up a telephone and discuss her situation with anyone, but the seed was sown. Many, many weeks later I left a Sands leaflet with Shirley, just for her to look at, nothing more.

As with all things, time marches on and Shirley was preparing to go back to work. Again the unknown, having to face people, comments, silence, again the courage that only most of us can dream about. Shirley, like Tim had done, took a deep breath and moved forward. That must have been the most difficult path to tread. The stress, exhaustion and anxiety-attacks to mention just a few agonies were all milestones that Shirley and Tim negotiated as each one presented itself. On top of all of that, Shirley had decided to recommence her studies for her dental nurse exam, due in May. This she negotiated with the determination and courage I was getting used to seeing manifest itself when hurdles needed to be got over. Suffice to say she passed the exam and she took a big step forward.

The day had also come when Shirley decided that contact with Sands would be a great benefit to herself and Tim. She still could not bring herself to pick up the telephone and call them. After a great deal of soul searching Shirley asked me to make the call for her from her home. This I did and explained the situation to the Sands representative. She fully understood Shirley's difficulty with making the call and promised to send more information but also gave the local contact numbers. When the time was right for Shirley and Tim they made contact with Sands, their benefit has been nothing but positive. Sands gave Shirley and Tim the opportunity of talking to bereaved parents who knew exactly how they felt and were able to support them through their pain but it could only happen when they felt ready.

Health visiting training prepares the fledgling HV 'to a point' and this is true of all trainings. Once qualified the 'professional' starts to really learn their job, hopefully appropriately mentored and supported by a trustworthy and supportive management structure. In reality, even though we will meet individuals who have lost an infant during a health visiting career, who can really be prepared within a professional training for grief and bereavement relating to a child? The theory might be there; it might be part of a module but then again it might not. Death is no stranger to nurses and all health visitors are nurses, (although that now is beginning to change with direct entry midwives being accepted for health visitor training), but an infant's death in the community is a different matter and one that demands some awareness and appropriate experience in nursing-related matters. After all you only have to look at all the advertising in society when all calendars, books, pictures and *expectation*s revolve around a bonny, happy thriving baby. There is only total shock when that doesn't happen and certainly no professional contingency plan.

Not all health visitors can respond to a bereavement situation. No one will ever find the situation easy but certain individuals within the profession will find the experience almost impossible to deal with. Remember all health professionals are also human and each individual's personal history could either enhance responses or make that response impossible. Even professionals have the 'right to pass', and that 'right to pass' should be respected by managers. However, that should not stop the finding of an appropriate professional to fill the gap. What is totally unacceptable is the attitude of 'nothing to do with us', 'what can we do?' or no contact is attempted at all.

Through my career, I have often stopped to wonder 'what exactly is a health visitor?'

The areas of work, expertise, training, and the professional 'tag' associated with the work. Sadly 'what do they do' is often a question directed at health visitors by members of the public and even more unsettling, colleagues in the nursing and medical professions.

Health visiting developed because of social concern and kindness, kindness being an ingredient that is vital to any caring profession. We might talk of progress, research based practice, technology and modern ways but without the caring ingredient health-visiting professionals become nothing more than empty vessels attempting to console and support individuals who are dealing with a type of pain that few of us can ever imagine what it must be like. It is probably old fashioned to say the words 'duty' these days, however that is still a word I am comfortable with, coupled with 'serving a community' because that is exactly what I believe health visitors should be doing. I make no apologies for saying this. I think in my profession you are sometimes challenged at all levels. Not only professionally but in human terms as well. It seems to occur more often than one might think.

After going back to work and having contact with Sands, Shirley's need for my visits slowly lessened but I was always available if she telephoned me. Sometimes I just called in, sometimes we talked on the telephone. Slowly Shirley found her strength and if I was needed she called. She knew nothing was too small, if she needed to talk she just rang. Things did present themselves over the months but with great courage Shirley faced each situation and I made myself as available as Shirley felt she needed me to.

One difficulty that emerged was the appointment to see the specialist who would discuss the possibility of future pregnancies. The situation was full of tension and fear of the unknown. I suggested that Shirley and Tim write a list of all the questions they had for the specialist to prevent them later driving away and then realising they had not asked a question that was important to them. The appointment took place and Shirley had the go ahead to try for another baby. Sadly she later miscarried at eight weeks. This was another loss bringing back memories and feelings that tear down confidence and drain away energy. When needed, Shirley rang me. That was and still is the understanding we have between us. Situations occurred every so often that caused Shirley great distress and confusion. Friendships could become strained because of a comment that pressed a button and produced painful memories, situations caused by people's reactions (and lack of them) led to more discomfort and confusion. It is fully understandable that grieving parents find it so difficult to go out for the most basic reasons, in case people's reactions cause more pain.

Through any year there are high days and holidays, birthdays to celebrate, times to get together. As the year progressed after the loss of Heulwen and headed for its closure, Christmas loomed. Any loss is often felt deeply at such a time, both by parents and the extended family. It is a very painful time for grieving parents as it reminds them of a loss, what might have been and emptiness. Basic reactions can be fraught with anxieties. How should they react? After all there are no guidelines as to how devastated parents should behave. Relax, have some amusing times, laugh and then feel guilty. Grief is a double-edged sword.

Anniversaries carry the same emotional charge and for some will continue to do so for the rest of their lives. Visits around these times can be very helpful but need to be carefully considered by any professional. Some people may not be able to cope with a visit; others may need a few visits to help them over the feelings that swamp them at that time. It is so important that it is understood that these feelings are normal and that nothing is going wrong. Shirley and I had many talks about anniversaries and holiday times and, as Shirley knew she could say exactly how she felt to me, I hope those times helped. I remember I had already warned her of the feelings that would almost invade her and Tim and that prevented too many surprises when they started to creep into their lives.

Routines and, hopefully some type of normality slides back into lives that have been in turmoil, back to work, out and about, meeting people. Routines that were in place before the bereavement appear and some sense of stability emerges. Shirley and Tim were doing ok.

Chapter 4
New Beginnings

One day Shirley rang me; I hadn't talked to her for a little while. She had called to tell me she was pregnant again.

One might think that a pregnancy would be the end of a chapter, the healing of a wound and a situation whereby everyone can again feel comfortable. How wrong that approach is. A further pregnancy spells, fear, terror and the crippling emotions that cause the first pregnancy and loss to be relived. This aspect is experienced in colour and in the most vivid terms. Happiness, terror and a relived tragedy are not a comfortable group of emotions to deal with.

It should be remembered that while a new pregnancy is, or should be, a trigger for celebration, in Shirley and Tim's case, it heralded fear and confusion. For most people it would be a time to be excited and tell friends and family. Shirley and Tim just wanted to sit quietly, tell no one and hope. A stillbirth and a miscarriage had not helped Shirley or Tim's confidence. In their own way they attempted to deal with the flood of emotions and anxieties by trying to insulate themselves from another possibly devastating disappointment.

Congratulations at that time would have been nothing but a double-edged sword. Shirley had to deal with going through the antenatal process again, meeting the midwives and specialists again. Meeting the people that had had some association with Heulwen brought back painful memories. It would also be a time when any badly thought out comment could cause indescribable pain and fear and possibly never be forgotten. I can remember many years ago a young mother in the same situation had been told that with another pregnancy she had been given a second chance, being that she had failed the first time. That comment made by a health professional will never be forgotten. *She had actually been told that she had failed after she had had a stillbirth.* That comment made by a health professional will never be forgotten.

Shirley contacted me herself when she was about twenty weeks pregnant. Although I already knew about the pregnancy, I had left Shirley to approach me. I was aware of the difficulties she would be facing and because of the relationship we had cultivated, I felt she would contact me when she was ready. Midwives do inform Health Visitors of a pending pregnancy at a certain time; this allows for good planning to take place before the antenatal visits from a Health Visitor. This is always a valuable time when relationships can be revived, renewed or commenced.

As soon as Shirley rang me I arranged to visit her at home. Shirley was wrestling with the emotions that had swamped both her and Tim. She was able to start talking about her feelings and fears and slowly we worked through them one by one. As we talked, so Shirley in turn talked to and supported Tim.

The new pregnancy called up all the old feeling and reminders of a bereavement. It was a time for reliving what had gone before. Shirley needed to know and be reassured that these were normal reactions, while I carefully monitored what was happening. In these situations it is not uncommon for 'parents to be' to try and disassociate themselves from the pregnancy, it is an attempt to deal with the pain and to try and buffer the fears. However these attempts can also produce feelings of guilt and more confusion. Questions can be asked as to 'how should we be reacting?' and 'are we rejecting this baby? By trying to disengage for a while. It must always be remembered that these feelings can be constant. They may switch on and off or occasionally appear. They can be there all the time, triggering highs and lows, feelings like depression, tears and despair. It is a constant wading through a mist of highly charged, potent emotions.

The expected baby can also be a focus of fears. Parent's reactions can be varied. Shirley confided in me that she was frightened that she would be able to love her new baby. She felt that perhaps all the traumas she and Tim had and were now going through might prevent her from bonding with her infant. She was also worried that some people might think her pregnancy was a replacement for Heulwen. I think some of these feelings eased a little when, after a scan, Shirley and Tim were told she was carrying a little boy.

I made myself available to Shirley as I had previously. I organised visits when she felt they were needed and remained at the end of the telephone when required. This allowed Shirley to be in complete control of our contact times. By doing that we met or talked when Shirley felt she needed to, rather than visiting occurring when a health professional thought it was right to do so. Her fears and feelings were talked about at length. It was so important to forewarn Shirley that the reactions she was dealing with were normal and that bereavement feelings can be recalled by a new pregnancy.

The birth of a new baby does not mean these feelings will disappear as other anxieties would probably take over and need to be dealt with. Grief does not have an on or off switch. Feelings that were thought to be worked through have a way of tapping you on the shoulder when you least expect them. They are often a lifelong companion but with time and practice, can be diluted and reorganised. But not usually discarded.

Many women that did not have the correct support after losing an infant are often caught up in the grieving process for the rest of their lives. On the surface such a person might appear to be coping well with life. More than likely you would never know what has happened in the past nor that the woman sitting next to you is longing for the child she lost years ago. Such individuals need a quality service that offers long term, appropriate support and care. Health Visitors have an important place within that remit though some might argue against that fact.

Shirley's antenatal care continued well. As the weeks passed there came a point when it was decided that she should have a caesarean. Tim was to be present and part of the birth and Shirley would have an epidural so she would be aware of everything going and not miss a moment of her baby's delivery.

Going into hospital produced extreme anxieties for both Shirley and Tim. Shirley later told me that she had arranged for her parents to also be there, *'just in case'* anything went wrong. Shirley was also helped greatly by her community midwife. The midwife had arranged to be at the delivery in the hospital and afterwards on the ward to look after her. This act showed the quality of care given to Shirley and extremes taken by some health professionals in an attempt to achieve it. I am proud to have her as my colleague.

While I understand the few days leading to the birth produced some worries, the day came and Charlie was born. The midwife was at the caesarean and looked after Shirley and Charlie afterwards. I was told very soon after the birth that all was well. After a few days and when Shirley was at home I rang her to arrange a visit.

Life settled into a gentle routine for Shirley and Tim. My first visit to see Shirley and Charlie was emotional for both of us especially when I was introduced to a beautiful little boy. Hurdles that presented themselves were discussed and dealt with. One had been the difficulty associated with Heulwen's bedroom, as it was now to be Charlie's in time. The feelings of somehow pushing Heulwen out or letting her down were talked about and as that did not have to happen immediately, time allowed Shirley and Tim to deal with it when they were ready.

Shirley struggled with confidence issues, she was in fact a mother experiencing new things and her anxieties were no different to any other new mother. However Shirley was also dealing with complete physical and emotional exhaustion linked to all the worries that had gone before.

Shirley had excellent instincts and as the days went on her confidence increased and Charlie, who was a very hungry baby, thrived. I visited very regularly and Shirley rang me when she had a query. I always told her that nothing was too small and just get in touch we would then work it out between us or I would call back in. The value of the support that I gave Shirley was that it led to her independence from, not dependence on, health professionals.

Routine health visiting became the norm. Shirley was a natural mother who, in spite of all her worries and anxieties bonded with Charlie beautifully. With her greatly increasing confidence developing it was like watching a bird getting ready to take its first flight. True to form she did just that, and she never looked back.

Chapter 5
Troubled Times

A few months down the line Shirley discovered she was pregnant again. Her pregnancy with Charlie had not been a joy in any sense mainly because of the worry associated with it. This pregnancy Shirley hoped to enjoy. Midwifery support was again engaged. The same lady would again be her community midwife. My routine visits continued as appropriate or when requested.

Shirley was soon to announce that they were moving house to a new area. She seemed satisfied that I would remain her health visitor. I was keen to remain so as I was aware that this pregnancy could still produce some anxieties related to past trauma. I hoped that continuity of care might help allay or resolve some of them.

I left Shirley and Tim to get on with their move and the pregnancy but was ready to respond to any queries or concerns. Sometimes there was a need to talk about Heulwen or Charlie or both, the new pregnancy and related hopes and fears. Time marched on and I was soon awaiting the news of a new baby.

The day came when the midwives let me know that Shirley had had a little boy by elective caesarean section and they had said that he had needed to go to Special Care Baby Unit for a while but that all now seemed well. He had come home with Shirley and Tim and the community midwives would now visit routinely until the day came for me to take over. I made a mental note that I would need to contact Shirley to arrange a visit in the next day or two now she was home but I would give her a little time to settle into her new routine first.

A few days later I enquired of the midwives how Shirley was doing to be told that Shirley's baby had become unwell and had been returned in an ambulance to the hospital where he had been born. With my heart in my throat I picked up the telephone with the intention of finding what was happening and to speak to Shirley if that was at all possible.

It has always been my policy as a practicing health visitor to make contact quickly with parents who have their babies or children admitted to hospital. In my view such contact not only produces a strong professional link to what is actually taking place but also extends the offer of support during difficult times for a family. It should always be remembered that the health visitor will be working with that family again in the future regardless of outcomes and such situations for a family produce feelings of being totally alone while experiencing extreme fear and distress because their child is ill.

Once I had tracked Shirley down the staff in the hospital brought her to the telephone to speak to me. I heard the voice that I had got to recognise well over the last few months. The voice was strained and shaking with distress. Shirley told me about her baby Joe's change when feeding and subsequent seizures, her rush to the hospital in an ambulance and that now baby Joe was fighting for his life. As best she could, Shirley went through all the procedures that had been put in place; her feelings and her fears. In the next few days Shirley and Tim were to experience sheer terror as they watched the doctors and nurses in the children's ward fight for Joe's life coupled with the loneliness of vigil and the feelings of being completely powerless.

I know that Shirley and Tim were fearful that the past was about to be revisited. Like them I felt powerless and that all I had to offer was a daily telephone call. I had given Shirley all the telephone numbers so she could contact me day or night. I also made it clear that if she would like me to come to the hospital I would be on my way. All she had to do was call.

During one telephone call, Shirley mentioned that her caesarean scar was uncomfortable. Being put in the position of having to rush Joe back to hospital her post operation care had been overlooked. I telephoned the midwives at the hospital and asked for their help. A midwife went to see Shirley in the children's ward to oversee all of Shirley's needs. Shirley was also expressing breast milk for Joe, so the support of a midwife at that time was so helpful. It was also someone who could keep an eye on all Shirley's health needs during such a difficult time.

As I write this I can see and feel the distress this evolving situation produced and my own anxiety levels increase just thinking about it. Imagine what a young family must go through. The fear that a baby might not 'make it'. The helplessness and reliance on strangers to 'make it all better'. Stressed families often describe explanations from the doctors and nurses as if the conversation is going on under water, words that don't quite make sense or sound clear. Sometimes it feels as if the whole world is moving in slow motion, coupled to the sights and sounds and smells of a high dependency unit, just more to add to the horror of the situation.

Each telephone call I made was heart wrenching. Shirley did her best to talk about what was happening. She and Tim had the full support of their extended family and as such little Charlie's needs were being met by careful and considered planning. Shirley managed to keep me updated daily when I rang. Joe seemed to be stabilizing and the seizures becoming fewer. Within a few days Shirley let me know that the decision had been made that he could be discharged with Shirley in charge of his medication: A frightening prospect for a young mother. I planned to be visiting within hours of his arrival at home and had reassured Shirley that we would deal with this next challenge together.

Some challenges in life are nothing short of being mountainous, have the accompanying feeling of being never ending and place a weight on vulnerable shoulders that most of us could not hope to carry. This was how I felt when Shirley opened the front door to me shortly after she returned home with Joe. Her pain hit me like a bolt of lightning and I wondered how I could possibly be any use to this young grieving woman and her family.

The practicalities of the situation had to be dealt with first. Controlling an infant's medication at home is a path laced with fear. Having to count seizures and sometimes miscount added to the feelings Shirley was grappling with of failure and fault. My visiting and availability offered to Shirley would, over the next months blow the word 'routine' out of the water. My visiting and availability however represented what Shirley and her family needed. I would be led by that need, be it a time to respond or withdraw, and not by what I as a health professional thought they needed.

Our relationship seemed to take on a different mantle. Issues relating to past, present *and* future surfaced and needed some consideration when time deemed it to be right.

Shirley began to be the real expert about Joe and all his needs. She became so finely tuned to medication requirements and recognition of seizures and their changes that I can only hold her in high regard. Shirley had also developed a sound working relationship with her paediatrician who she calls doctor M. Having worked with him before I knew he would advise, support and encourage her in a careful and kindly way. To say this man is worth gold dust is to put it mildly.

Issues that Shirley found difficult to deal with popped up to the surface regularly. She had to battle with feelings of failure relating to Joe and his seizures and that was compounded by the strong re-emergence of grief relating to Heulwen. In modern language, 'a double whammy'. The word 'fault' raised its head and caused much heartbreak. 'Fault' had no place in the scenario but it took some time for Shirley to be able to accept that. These strong feelings create devastation within a family. Feelings not acknowledged, not spoken, have a way of developing a distance between individuals within a family, be it nuclear or extended. Shirley, while carrying the burdens placed upon her always stayed concerned for Tim and Charlie's needs. We talked about them frequently. It should always be remembered that the feelings that surface would need to be dealt with at some time. Quick and thoughtless comments only add to the despair. Again, like before, it was a time when friendships, associations and just the simple procedure of going shopping becomes a minefield of pain, anger and total turmoil.

Shirley from early on was battling complete exhaustion. Sleep deprivation is one of the most malevolent situations to be in, coupled with the 24/7 care that Joe needed while trying to keep a balance for Tim and Charlie produced an almost impossible situation to manage. However, this is what Shirley battled with day in and day out. Appointments that Joe needed to attend could only produce anxieties. Constant weight checks were needed to enable the appropriate medication to be given. One thing after another. When the time seemed right, I suggested that Shirley see her counsellor again. This would offer a greater in-depth assistance and guidance through all Shirley's feelings and issues. Shirley agreed and an appointment was set up.

Months passed and Shirley had dealt with all her family's needs marvellously. Joe's fits were slightly less and Shirley was recognising that she was getting control of the situation. At a later date the drugs were changed and slowly the seizures became less with some free times.

Every so often Shirley would need to talk about the time since Joe's birth. It had been a time that felt like she was being pushed along at a great speed totally out of control while being surrounded by unimaginable fears. Now Shirley worried that she had missed so much in relation to Joe and his growing up as life had been so intense. Priorities had demanded that she focus on other things. Charlie's needs also raised some anxieties and Shirley worried that she had neglected him because of the intensity of Joe's needs. In fact she had been sensitive to all those things while carrying so much agony herself.

Time, as it does marched on. A year had passed and Shirley looked to bringing more balance to the family's life. Going back to work was one thing that happened. As Shirley had been the only one to cope with Joe's needs for so long, she experienced a considerable internal wrestling match before she was able to leave Joe with someone else. Slowly her confidence in the people she had chosen for this task increased and all was to be well. That had been a very hard hurdle to get over for Shirley. Joe's needs still dictated the need for many appointments for check-ups and that did result in Shirley giving up work at a later date so as not to be considered an unreliable employee. Life still threw up swings and roundabouts that needed uncomfortable and unwanted decisions.

Before we knew it Joe was eighteen months. Over that time his development checks had shown he was a little behind in some areas but as time went on some of the gaps were closing. Whatever Joe had needed in encouragement to achieve, Shirley and Tim had made sure he had received. That had produced a very outward looking little boy with great courage, who would have a go at most things and one who had a tremendously cheeky character. Joe's loving big brother Charlie was also a great assistance to Joe and to this day they are very close and considerate of each other. Shirley also had a supportive and caring family around her that helped whenever they could.

My involvement with Shirley lessened as things became more balanced. She always knew how to contact me if I was needed. Because of Shirley's great courage and determination, we found ourselves again at the juncture that I visited if Shirley called me. She had become the true expert on her own child and had a sound relationship with her paediatrician who she trusted completely. There are times when all beautiful birds should spread their wings and fly and Shirley was doing just that.

Chapter 6
Health Visitor / Health Visiting

The health-visiting role has the ability to change and develop according to a need required at that time. Individuals are just that, individuals; and patterns of care or care plans must be 'moulded' to each persons or family's specific requirements. My role as a health visitor in Shirley's and her family's life was to change again. I have always felt that parents become the experts on their own children. Shirley had definitely become just that. Charlie and Joe's needs were completely met, understood and controlled by Shirley. She had excellent relationships with the health professionals at consultant level and knew when and how to respond to any change that demanded immediate attention. Caring for Joe and any extended situations that Joe became involved with like mother and toddler groups or play groups were thoroughly researched and advised as to Joe's needs before he was allowed to attend. The knowledge and control that Shirley developed allowed her to become very independent and secure within her own right. In time this was to lead to a great involvement with Sands and a very positive view of the world.

My role, quite rightly became quietly supportive. Situations requiring advice or contact on difficult days were now under Shirley's control. She just rang me when she needed to have some contact. As in all things, there were good days and bad days, I was available if needed and while this situation continued for a very long time, the aim was always to encourage Shirley's independence to be able to function within a very difficult and frightening situation.

The time came when due to a house and area move Shirley's health visitor would also need to change. I visited her to explain this as moves like this can produce great insecurities when having to meet a new person, 'a stranger', in Shirley's view. I had made contact with Shirley's new health visitor asking her to make contact and introduce herself. As it was only seven miles away I suggested a joint visit might help the changeover. Sadly that didn't happen. Shirley remained registered with the doctors I was attached to so some contact would occur and if all else failed Shirley knew how to contact me.

Changes like this do occur within caseloads. It should be remembered that after such traumatic times, changes of any sort can resurrect old fears and insecurities until a relationship with 'the new' professional is developed. At the time of the change Joe was old enough that within the 'normal' health visiting protocols, he did not require regular contact. However trauma is no respecter of protocols and the 'moulding' of individual care packages is well within the remit of the health visiting service.

Shirley and I maintained a contact and this led to me being asked to join her at a Sands conference in Powys. We presented a workshop that went through Shirley's experiences and the value of the health visiting service in these circumstances. Professionals and Sands supporters were there. What struck me was the number of women who came who had lost infants years ago, one in particular who was still grieving because she had never had anyone to talk to and who had had a stillbirth thirty years ago. Her pain and anguish was all consuming all these years later. (Others had similar stories to tell, to our shame). That lady I will never forget in fact something she and Shirley said made me suggest to Shirley after the workshop, that we should think of writing a book.

In 2009 I was asked by Sands to accompany Shirley to London to speak at a conference. Its title was Uncertainty and Loss in Maternity and Neonatal Care. Again Shirley and I delivered 'our story' to an audience of Midwives, Health Visitors, Sands supporters and other health professionals. The response to us was very interesting in that in a time of increased technology, budget cuts and increased paperwork, people still value 'the human touch' but find they do not always have the time to deliver it. Something we should perhaps be thinking about.

I look back over the years that I have known Shirley and her family. I see a broken heart mended in such a way as to now have the ability to help others. 'The boys' are just that, boys being boys, a family that has drawn strength from battling adversity.

Reflection is a great thing, a valuable tool for any health professional and one I use a great deal. Looking back allows me to be critical of my reactions and input but also critical of the availability (or not) of the type of support I could have found useful in a personal capacity while dealing with such a traumatic incident within my caseload. Too often health visitors are left to 'talk amongst themselves' when a more skilled support or debriefing facility is required. However when the actual health visiting training does not give time to even discussing the possibility that within every career a stillbirth could occur, it should not be a surprise that there are few postgraduate training opportunities or workshops to raise awareness of the needs for both family or the health professional. The awareness raising is left to charities such as Sands with the hope that the knowledge and wisdom within their ranks filters down to those dealing with the situations within the field of delivery of care. Perhaps Sands and all universities that train health visitors should develop a partnership to ensure the fledgling health visitors are prepared appropriately. One hopes that such a partnership will blossom in the future.

It is interesting that in the main, health visitors are 'left to it'. Management have staffing levels, budgets and the introduction of yet more technology to think about. Training involving something that might happen is not high on any agenda. However the failure of delivering appropriate care to a family that has suffered a stillbirth has repercussions that can echo through decades and cast a shadow over any subsequent plans that family might have when a new baby is planned. In short, the delivery of good sensitive and appropriate care to a family is cost effective and produces a benefit to all parties concerned. Grieving mothers who have had bad experiences from health professionals tell the truth. They do not misinterpret the situation and any management that thinks they do need to reassess their attitudes. A statement like, 'I know you haven't got a baby but would you like me to visit?' has no place within a caring profession. Such statements are said to all our shame and really do occur.

Appropriate training is the key to good health care delivery. Counselling foundation workshops within health visitor training would sow the seed for further development of the post-graduate once they are working in the field. It would also benefit the practitioner in all areas of their health visiting practice. Experienced, trustworthy supervision / counselling should also be available to all practitioners who have such traumatic situations within their caseloads. Again, to benefit all individuals concerned and assist good delivery of care.

I acknowledge that staffing levels, budgets and corporate caseloads of 600 for one health visitor in some areas of the UK reduce health visiting to 'fire fighting' situations suggesting that any extras added to already stretched services would sink the boat. But one aspect of health care delivery that is free and available to all practitioners is 'the human touch', a vital ingredient when dealing with such trauma and grief within a family. Technology will not help health professionals deliver the care at source. It might be useful to inform and guide practice if sound research papers are read and practitioners are allowed to develop their skills through appropriate training, if made available. But when you are sitting opposite a grieving mother who is consumed with pain, your own training and experience are the key ingredients to assist the situation not the latest computer or smart phone.

I feel we are at a time when health professionals are begging to be listened to in relation to workloads, training availabilities and their own needs as human beings. After the conference in London this was confirmed to me in very strong terms. Health professionals want to deliver care at the highest level possible but many feel they have their hands tied by protocols and targets that are deemed to be more important. I strongly feel that 'the human touch' has to be part of the care given to families who suffer the loss of an infant. Health professionals should not be afraid of 'the human touch', as is does not compromise practice, it enhances it. However if we lose 'the human touch' while delivering health care, then I am sure we as health professionals have a great deal to fear not only for our practice but for the future of our profession.

Being Shirley's health visitor through extreme trauma and pain over the years has taught me a great deal about my profession and about myself. It has been an honour. They all will have a place in my heart forever.

Sands
Stillbirth & neonatal death charity

Sands, the stillbirth and neonatal death charity was founded in 1978 by a small group of bereaved parents devastated by the death of their babies, and by the total lack of acknowledgement and understanding of the significance and impact of their loss.

Since that time we have supported many thousands of families whose babies have died, offering emotional support, comfort and practical help.

Sands today operates throughout the UK and focuses on three main areas of work:

We support anyone affected by the death of a baby

Bereavement support is at the core of everything we do. Some of the services that we offer include:

- Helpline for parents, families, carers and health professionals

- UK-wide network of support Groups with trained befrienders

- Online forum and message-boards enabling bereaved families to connect with others

- Website and a wide range of leaflets, books and other resources.

We work in partnership with health professionals to try to ensure that bereaved parents and families receive the best possible care

We undertake a comprehensive programme of training, workshops and talks for health professionals based on the Sands Guidelines which give practical guidance on how to meet parents' needs and provide good care.

We promote and fund research that could help to reduce the loss of babies' lives

In spite of medical advances, the shocking reality is that each day in the UK there are ten babies who are stillborn and seven who die within the first 28 days of life. Through our Why17? campaign, we are raising vital funds for research, while challenging the Government to address these individual tragedies as a matter of urgency and priority.

We depend on the extraordinary energies of our supporters to raise the £1.5 million that we need to deliver the wide range of services that we offer.

If you would like any further information or support please contact us or visit our website.

Support: 020 7436 5881   helpline@uk-sands.org
Enquiries: 020 7436 7940 info@uk-sands.org
Website: www.uk-sands.org
                www.why17.org

Write to us: Sands, 28 Portland Place, London W1B 1LY

Charity Registration Number: 299679 | Company Limited by Guarantee Number: 2212082

Lightning Source UK Ltd.
Milton Keynes UK
UKOW040431160911

178771UK00001B/33/P